THE REAL
REVOLUTION

THE REAL REVOLUTION

The Global Story
of American Independence

MARC ARONSON

CLARION BOOKS ❀ NEW YORK

To the real revolution in our lives, Raphael Kabir Aronson.
You are making the world anew for Sasha, for Marina, and for me.
And to the memory of John Stix,
whose companionship meant so much to my mother.

Clarion Books
a Houghton Mifflin Company imprint
215 Park Avenue South, New York, NY 10003
Copyright © 2005 by Marc Aronson

The text was set in 14-point Fournier.
Book design by Trish Parcell Watts.
Maps on pages 40–41, 52, 53, and 110 by Kayley LeFavier.

www.houghtonmifflinbooks.com

Printed in the United States.

Library of Congress Cataloging-in-Publication Data
Aronson, Marc.
The real revolution : the global story of American independence / by Marc Aronson.
p. cm.
Includes index.
ISBN 0-618-18179-2
1. United States—History—Revolution, 1775–1783—Causes—Juvenile literature.
2. United States—Politics and government—To 1775—Juvenile literature.
3. Great Britain—Politics and government—1760–1789—Juvnile Literature.
4. World politics—18th century. 5. Globilization—Juvenile literature. I. Title.
E210.A76 2005
973.3—dc22   2005001088

ISBN-13: 978-0-618-18179-7
ISBN-10: 0-618-18179-2

MP 10 9 8 7 6 5 4 3 2

Contents

Acknowledgments

I am especially grateful to readers who have gone out of their way to help me formulate my ideas and shape them into this book. Dr. Thomas Bender was the model of a dissertation adviser for me in graduate school and, these many years later, an engaged critic of this book. Virginia Buckley always challenges me. Renée Cafiero keeps me honest; Trish Parcell and Joann Hill know how to make a beautiful book. My thanks to Lynne Polvino at Clarion for her attention to innumerable details. Peter Dimock was encouraging when I needed it. Vicki Smith caught me every time I was napping at the keyboard; she sent librarians throughout the state of Maine scrambling to check a (misleading) fact. Martin Durrant at the Victoria & Albert Museum in London was most helpful when a harried American showed up unannounced in his office. Moi Tu, Julia Eisen, and Martin Minz of the British Library sorted through a barrage of e-mails to help me make sense of their procedures. Thanks to Minu Tharoor and her sons, Ishaan and Kanishk, for reporting to me about their recent visit to Plassey. My wife and soon-to-be coauthor, Marina Budhos, led me to learn more about India; she never lets me settle for an average expression where there is an exciting one waiting to be discovered.

I would also like to thank Tess and Jake Weiss for being such great pals for my son Sasha, and another neighbor, Jim Murphy, for sharing books and being the most helpful and generous reader.

Cast of Characters

THE BRITISH

HISTORICAL FIGURES

Queen Elizabeth
Sir Walter Ralegh
James I
Charles I
Charles II
Philip Amadas
Arthur Barlowe
Oliver Cromwell
William and Mary

EAST INDIA COMPANY

Robert, Lord Clive, Baron of Plassey
Margaret, née Maskelyne, his wife
John Z. Holwell
Laurence Sulivan
Stringer Lawrence
Job Charnock

THE JOHNSTONE CLAN

Patrick Johnstone
John Johnstone, Member of Parliament
George Johnstone, Member of Parliament
William Pulteney, born Johnstone, Member of Parliament
James Johnstone
James Murray, first cousin

MEMBERS OF PARLIAMENT

John Montagu, Earl of Sandwich
John Wilkes
Colonel John Burgoyne

KING AND MINISTERS

John Stuart, Earl of Bute
George Grenville
Charles Watson-Wentworth, Marquess of Rockingham
William Pitt, Earl of Chatham
Charles Townshend
Wills Hill, Lord Hillsborough
Frederick, Lord North
King George III
William, Duke of Cumberland, brother of George II

ABOLITIONISTS

William Wilberforce
John Newton
Thomas Clarkson
Zachary Macaulay
Thomas Babington
George Whitefield

CAST OF CHARACTERS

BANKER

Alexander Fordyce

NINETEENTH-CENTURY FIGURES

Thomas Babington Macaulay
Queen Victoria
Benjamin Disraeli

SOLDIERS FIGHTING IN AMERICA

General Edward Braddock
Captain Robert Stobo
Major General James Wolfe
Major Isaac Barré
Major General Jeffrey Amherst
Colonel Simeon Ecuyer
Charles, Marquis Cornwallis
General John Forbes

COMMENTATOR

Horace Walpole

THE FRENCH

Joseph-François Dupleix
Marquis Louis-Joseph de Montcalm

THE AMERICANS

HISTORICAL FIGURES

Anne Hutchinson
John Winthrop

EIGHTEENTH-CENTURY COLONISTS

George Washington
Lawrence Washington, his half brother
Thomas Jefferson
Thomas Walker
Daniel Boone
John Findley
James Otis Sr.
James Otis Jr.
John Adams
Patrick Henry
Benjamin Franklin
Oxenbridge Thacher
Ebenezer MacIntosh
Reverend Jonathan Mayhew
John Dickinson
Samuel Adams
John Hancock
George Mason
Richard Henry Lee
Dr. Benjamin Rush
Thomas Paine

OFFICIALS

Francis Bernard
Thomas Hutchinson
Andrew Oliver

AMERICAN INDIANS

Tanaghrisson
Neolin
Pontiac
Captain Will

CAST OF CHARACTERS

TWENTIETH-CENTURY LEADERS

Dr. Martin Luther King Jr.
Cesar Chavez

THE EAST INDIANS

Omichand

BENGALIS

Siraj Ud-Daula, nawab
Mir Jafar, nawab

MOGUL EMPERORS

Shah Alam II
Babur
Akbar

TWENTIETH-CENTURY LEADER

Mohandas K. Gandhi

To My Readers

This book offers a new way of looking at the events that led up to the American Revolution. I am about to take you back to the 1700s, and around the world, and show that charging war elephants attacking a crumbling fort in India, and the high-stakes gambles of bankers in Scotland, were as important to the pathway to American independence as patriot leaders and British laws. What you read here may be unfamiliar, but it is all true, and it is a past that makes sense to me—a past in which global connections were as important as they are now. Even if you disagree with me, that's good, because it will mean you have your own strong sense of American history. That is as it should be. While we need to be good researchers, the past we are likely to believe is one that sounds right to us in the present.

Some of the ideas expressed here are so new that the scholarly books that explore them in detail are just now being written—I describe that research in my notes, so if you, your teachers, or any other readers have questions about what is written here, you can see how I developed my ideas. I believe young people should have access to the latest historical insights—ideas that reflect their own times. One of the most important of these new approaches is what is called "transnational" history. These historians seek to move past the stories of separate nations and instead to trace the ways in which interconnected events unfolded all around the world. Writing this book gave me the great pleasure of passing along some of their new ideas and insights to you.

Those of you who have read my previous books on Sir Walter Ralegh and on John Winthrop and Oliver Cromwell will have some advantage here, as themes and incidents in those books influenced the people in this one. Taken together, the three books are three acts in the unfolding saga of the period between the first English explorations of the New World and the birth of the United States. But I have written each one so that it can stand alone. If you like reading about familiar heroes such as George Washington and Samuel Adams and not poet explorers such as Ralegh or great generals like Oliver Cromwell, you can stick by your preferences. I happen to like the long-unfolding plot lines in epics: small foreshadowed hints that later build to climactic moments.

When did the American Revolution begin? That is another way of asking, When did Americans know that they needed to live under their own government? When did they become so certain of this belief that they were willing to die to defend it? This is a crucial question for Americans, perhaps the most important one in all our history. If we know what made the founders of this nation decide that they were no longer British, we can describe at least the initial push, the starting momentum, for what we are now.

John Adams looked back on this question in an 1815 letter to Thomas Jefferson. His famous words helped me to define what this book is about: "What do we mean by the Revolution? The war? That was no part of the Revolution; it was only an effect and consequence of it. The Revolution was in the minds of the people, and this was effected from 1760 to 1775."

What was this revolution in the "minds of the people"? Of course it involved the famous ideas about liberty and familiar protests about taxation covered in this and every other book. But there is a missing part of that story, which has never been described to young readers. Ironically, America became an independent nation because of connections that linked together people, ideas, and goods all over the world.

Anyone who reads about the events leading up to the American Revolution quickly recognizes that the Boston Tea Party marked a key turning point, after which the momentum for war accelerated in both England and America. I began my research for this book by asking a simple question: "Why tea?" Why did tea matter so much to the English that they would insist on selling it to the Americans, even at the risk of encouraging the colonials to feel more rebellious, more independent? Why was it so important to the colonials not to accept the tea that they would risk being crushed by the most powerful army in the world?

I knew the familiar phrases about taxation and representation, but not why tea became the center of the controversy. Most books answer that question by mentioning the financial problems of the East India Company. But why was that company in so much trouble? Very few explain that. This one does, and researching it changed everything I thought I knew about American history.

The story of the Revolution begins in battle, with three men-at-arms. One will lose; one will die; one will gain an empire.

THREE SOLDIERS

Robert Clive,

George Washington,

and James Wolfe

CHAPTER 1

First Soldier:
From Despair to Conquest

EXILE IN MADRAS

The school, the town, the life he was leading had nothing to offer Robert Clive. Born in 1725 in the tiny village of Moreton in the center of England, he was the kind of boy who was always getting into fights—when he wasn't organizing other boys into gangs for the fun of terrorizing people or shaking them down for a little money. He was a bully aching for the challenge that would make him a man, and his belligerence was a reflection of his father's frustration.

During the English Civil War Robert's great-grandfather had fought beside Oliver Cromwell as one of his fierce mounted "ironsides," and the Clives had been leading lights of their community for centuries. But they were not wealthy. This was particularly hard to take, as England was becom-

William Hogarth engraved "Gin Lane" in 1751. At the time, one out of every six houses in this very poor neighborhood near Covent Garden sold cheap gin, and London's desperate poor were literally drinking themselves to death. Hogarth was both a talented artist and a sharp social satirist, and this image helped draw attention to the miserable lives people lived in the wealthy city.

(PAULSON 186 (111), THE BRITISH MUSEUM)

ing a land of the very rich and the very poor. Good old families like the Clives had the nauseating sense that they were slipping—no longer honored for their past glories, not able to keep up with their more fortunate peers.

While nobles were building magnificent palaces such as Houghton Hall and Blenheim Palace, London was filling with poor people who were killing themselves by drinking cheap gin. Prostitution was common in London, and everything up to and including a seat in Parliament was for sale—if you had the money. As the famous diplomat and lover Casanova put it, "In London, everything is easy to him who has money and is not afraid to spend it." Robert's father trained as a lawyer, but he was not earning enough to become a member of Parliament, or to have a fine home, which left him feeling less and less secure and important. He could not afford to have a wild son who resisted discipline follow him into his profession. Through connections he instead got the seventeen-year-old Robert a job with the East India Company. Shipped off to India, Robert would, at best, return home relatively well off in twenty years or so. At worst, he would die, as did the majority of those posted to Calcutta.

"You'll make it, son, or you'll die," Robert's father seemed to be saying to him. "I can't do anything for you here, and I won't have you hanging around making trouble."

The East India Company that Clive joined is one of history's most fascinating disappearing acts. From his day through the middle of the nineteenth century it was legendary for its wealth and power. Decorated with murals showing its ships proudly sailing to distant ports, its headquarters on Leadenhall Street in London were a symbol of its global reach. Today the company and its offices are gone, its vast warehouses put to other uses. It is as if a business that seems completely dominant today, such as Microsoft,

The headquarters of the East India Company on Leadenhall Street in London at the time Robert Clive joined the firm. The large murals of Indiamen—company ships—the proud insignia, and the ornamental fish show a dynamic company on the rise. (P2167, COURTESY THE BRITISH LIBRARY).

simply vanished. Impossible as it would have seemed to anyone at the time, the ill-at-ease seventeen-year-old would be instrumental in the company's triumph—and its demise.

The company made its fortunes in Asian trade, and the Indian subcontinent provided a perfect location for its business. Situated between the Arabian Sea, which made for easy connections with traders in the Middle East, and the Bay of Bengal, which provided an open sea to the Spice Islands, and on to China and Japan, India was an ideal stopping place for merchants. India itself produced an astonishing variety of valuable fabrics. To this day the names of many cotton and silk textiles show their Indian origin, such as calico (originally from Calicut, on the southwestern coast), muslin, dungaree, gingham, seersucker, and, of course, madras. (For a map of India, see page 110.)

The company was founded in 1600, just as Sir Walter Ralegh tried to plant settlers at Roanoke and John Smith helped another colony to survive at Jamestown. Sending colonists to America and establishing trading posts in Asia were part of the same English push to reach out into the world. But India was very different from America. For one thing, Europeans were more likely to die from Indian diseases than Indians were from European. Since the Indians were still dominant in their homelands, the company merchants were completely dependent on India's rulers for everything—even permission to buy, sell, and trade.

Fortunately for the English, they arrived during one of those moments that often appear in fantasy novels when an old empire is dying and, in the chaos, strange new alliances are formed.

In the early sixteenth century the conquering armies of the Muslim emperor Babur swept into India. He and his heirs expanded their Mogul (sometimes spelled Moghul or Mughal) empire until it controlled much of the subcontinent. The Moguls created a wealthy dynasty that built the Taj Mahal, and Akbar, who lived in the age of England's Queen Elizabeth, was the wisest, most able ruler anywhere on earth. But by the eighteenth century their hold on power was weakening, and in every region local leaders juggled alliances, hoping to hold on to or expand their power, while awaiting the fate of the empire.

At first the English hardly counted in these calculations. The Moguls granted the company only three headquarters, or "presidencies," on the vast subcontinent. On the northwestern coast, facing the Arabian Sea, they had access to Bombay (now officially called Mumbai). Madras (now Chennai), which was considered relatively healthy for Europeans, and Calcutta (now Kolkata), which was not, were the places where an enterprising young man could be sent to make his fortune. The change in the names of these three cities is part of the same story as the disappearance of the East India Company—to many modern Indians the company is a bad memory best forgotten. Clive, as much as anyone, is responsible for this legacy. He is the symbol of the unhappy era of English rule. (For the location of the three presidencies, see the map on page 110.)

Clive was sent to Madras. Located on India's southeastern coast, facing the waters of the Bay of Bengal, Madras was the East India Company's first toehold on the subcontinent. Working there was a misery for company men. They sweltered through hot, sultry days whose lowest temperatures were higher than anything they had experienced at home—March days could reach into the hundreds—and monsoon-driven rains in October and November brought torrential downpours. One English traveler described the air as "so intensely hot that I could compare it only to standing within the oppressive influence of the steam of a furnace." As late as the nineteenth century, ice was transported in the holds of ships all the way from New England to cool company employees.

In 1640 the company started creating a massive walled complex called Fort St. George, which gave its employees a world of their own. When Clive arrived in Madras more than a hundred years later, it was still not finished. Despite all this construction, Madras had no port to speak of. Ships had to cast their anchors into the choppy waters offshore, where they might be battered by monsoon winds. Then small boats would row out to bring passengers through the crashing surf to the shore. Knocked about, half dizzy, only

This painting of a typical Madras departure gives a sense of the rolling waves and the choppy passage between ship and shore.   (P1552, COURTESY THE BRITISH LIBRARY)

to be left in foul streets and the baking, blasting heat, everyone hated landing in Madras. Still, it was a very profitable place for the company to do business.

In the villages nearby, weavers spun cotton that traders sold to the English. Boats sailing along the coast also brought finished fabrics such as chintz to Madras. Some of these well-crafted, beautiful fabrics were purchased for sale in England, while others were transferred to ships headed east to what is now Indonesia, where they were traded for spices. The Madras trade even reached as far as China, where the English bought tea in exchange for products such as Indonesian copper and sugar.

It is not hard to imagine what Clive must have seen and felt when he arrived. When he began walking the dusty streets, he would immediately have been overwhelmed by the strangeness of the world that was now his home. The many Hindu temples could only have seemed pagan—a sign of being a world away from anything familiar. On the streets he would have seen only men—since this was a Muslim-ruled area, very few women appeared in public. For a young man who had lived his entire life on an island where most people were fair, the wide variety of dark-skinned people he now passed would have been a constant reminder that he was a complete outsider. Clive's situation was all the worse because the East India Company was a rigid, status-conscious, cliquish world, and he had no entry into its inner circle.

Robert Clive was exiled from his family and his homeland, at the very bottom of his employer's social scale, and isolated in an alien world. To complete this bleak picture, he was not making enough money to cover basic expenses and was soon in debt.

Writing home to a cousin, he admitted that "I have not enjoyed one happy day since I left my native country." Though he was close to his mother, no one in his family responded. Anyone might have found that silence devastating, but Clive often experienced emotional ups and downs with an extreme intensity similar to the mood swings of the great Puritan general Oliver Cromwell. According to a secondhand account that most of his biographers trust, Clive could not endure living another day: Apparently he twice played a kind of Russian roulette, aiming a partially loaded pistol at his head and pulling the trigger.

Suicide loomed over Clive as a last resort, a way out when there was no possibility of improving his life. But when he survived the gunplay, he began to believe that "fate must be reserving me for some purpose." Staying away from the other hard-drinking, brawling junior employees, he turned to study. He scoured the company library and began forming a sense of his possible future from books such as Sir Walter Ralegh's *History of the World*. Just as with Cromwell, the knife edge for Clive was between hopeless, helpless despair and a sense of purpose that made him feel he was the servant of destiny.

THE IMPOSSIBLE SIEGE

Destiny appeared in Clive's life in the form of the French. Two years after he arrived in India, the French captured Madras, and the young Englishman barely escaped from the city by disguising himself as an Indian. That humiliating exit was Clive's first clash with one of his great rivals, J. F. Dupleix, who was the best, and most farsighted, European leader on the subcontinent. Dupleix was determined not only to ruin the British East India

Above: *The East India Company purchased painted and dyed cotton, called chintz, near Madras and transported it to England, where there were many eager customers. Painted around 1800 in the same region of India, this image shows a merchant selling bolts of chintz. This style of painting is called tanjore,* and artists who used the method included actual gold leaf and sometimes semi-precious stones in their art.   (ADD.OR.2531, COURTESY THE BRITISH LIBRARY)

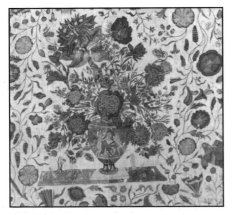

Left: *Chintz was often dyed a vivid red called East India Madder and then used to upholster furniture. The birds and flowers in this piece are all a rich red.*   (CT28769, V&A IMAGES/VICTORIA AND ALBERT MUSEUM)

Opposite: *Villages near Madras produced beautiful finished fabrics that the company purchased to resell throughout Asia and Europe. A large* palampore *such as this, which could be used as a bedcover or wall hanging, was popular in England. The design was sewn with silk thread on a cotton background. This* palampore *was made around the time Clive arrived in India.*

(CT23087, V&A IMAGES/VICTORIA AND ALBERT MUSEUM)

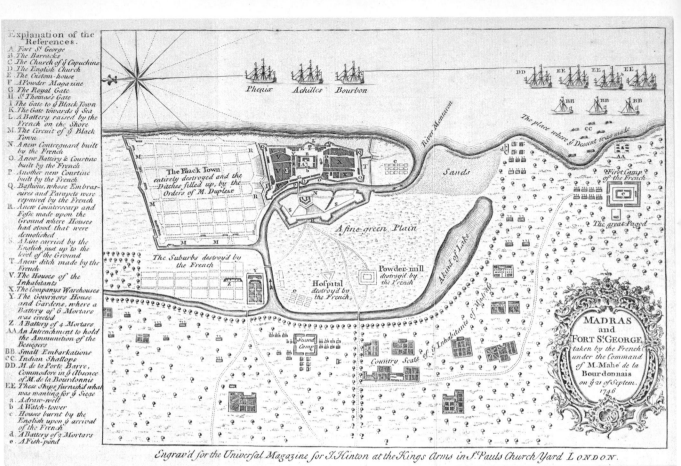

The Black Town entirely destroyed and the Ditches filled up, by the Orders of M. Dupleix

Phenix   Achilles   Bourbon

River Montaigne

The place where ye Descent was made

Sands

A fine green Plain

A kind of Lake

First Camp of the French

The great Pagod

The Suburbs destroy'd by the French

Hospital destroy'd by the French

Powder-mill destroyd by the French

Country Seats of ye Inhabitants of Madras

Island Camp

MADRAS and FORT St GEORGE, taken by the French under the Command of M. Mahé de la Bourdonnais on ye 21 of Septem. 1746.

Engrav'd for the Universal Magazine for J. Hinton at the Kings Arms in St Pauls Church Yard LONDON.

The French attack on Madras. If you look closely at this map, it describes "the black town"—the Indian area—as "entirely destroyed" by Dupleix. This map and the accompanying legend spell out the entire story of the French triumph. Clive barely escaped, in disguise. The large building next to "the black town" is Fort St. George. (P232, COURTESY THE BRITISH LIBRARY)

J. F. Dupleix had ambitious plans for the French East India Company and for France's role in India. Had he defeated Clive, the subsequent history of India, and for that matter, of Europe and North America, could have been completely different. For one thing, the book you are reading now might be in French.

(P1467, COURTESY THE BRITISH LIBRARY)

Company but to win an empire in India for himself and for France. Dupleix worked for the French East India Company. Even though the English, French, and Dutch East India companies had similar names, they were actually the bitterest of rivals. Rumor had it that Dupleix had already received a king's ransom in money and jewels from Indian princes eager to side with him in his campaigns.

Beyond what he had learned through the escapades of his band of schoolboys, Clive had no military training. He did not see himself as a professional soldier. But he was a determined man seeking a scope of action, and if fighting could give him a way to make his name, he would eagerly take the challenge. He volunteered to join in the contest against the French and was given a commission as an ensign. He soon acquired something even more important: a mentor. If Clive's life were to be fictionalized as an epic quest in the *Lord of the Rings, Sword in the Stone* model, this would be the moment when the Gandalf, Merlin character appeared.

In 1748 a retired captain named Stringer Lawrence was sent to India to take charge of the troops who still held a fort near Madras. Though Lawrence was overweight and hardly looked the part of a solider, he had the best military mind of the English in India; he and Clive soon recognized in each other a kind of battle-born father-son team. Lawrence appreciated Clive's dash and energy; Clive was,

Stringer Lawrence did not look like a tough, disciplined soldier, but that is exactly what he was. In Lawrence, Clive found the perfect inspiring, guiding, challenging mentor he needed. Lawrence was painted by Thomas Gainsborough, who specialized in making portraits of important people.

(NPG777, COURTESY THE NATIONAL PORTRAIT GALLERY, LONDON)

perhaps for the first time, able to accept an older man's discipline and greater knowledge. Three years later he had his first great chance to show what he had learned.

After a treaty was signed in 1748 that returned Madras to the English, England and France were officially at peace and Clive left active service. But Lawrence helped him to land a job as quartermaster, which paid exceptionally well—since it was expected that he would receive a payoff for every single item he bought. Then, in 1750, France and England backed rival Indian claimants to an area near Madras. By the following summer Clive had again volunteered to join the army and to lead a diversionary attack that could help decide the contest. It did more than that, for his leadership in the siege of Arcot made him into a legend.

Clive at Arcot is to the English what Davy Crockett at the Alamo would be to Americans—had Davy not only survived and won but gone on single-handedly to conquer Mexico. Clive led about two hundred Europeans and six hundred Indians to take the fort of Arcot. The nineteenth-century English author Thomas Babington Macaulay lived in India not long after Clive's day, and he wrote an engaging account of his life that was a favorite for generations of English and American readers. The writing is still vivid, though it is filled with the ideas and judgments of a long-past era. As Macaulay described it, "The weather was stormy; but Clive pushed on, through thunder, lightning, and rain, to the gates of Arcot."

Though eleven hundred soldiers massed behind the red-clay walls of the fort, they were intimidated by news of the rigid discipline of Clive's men, who had marched through a raging storm. The entire army fled before engaging Clive in battle. Clive installed his own men in their place. As Clive hoped, the Indian leader allied with the French was alarmed at this and

Elephants went into battle covered in this armor. The shaffron, *which covers the elephant's head and reaches halfway down his trunk, was made of 2,195 plates woven together in columns. The complete armor consisted of 8,439 plates, of which 5,840 survive. This armor was brought to England from India by Robert Clive's daughter-in-law; only one other set of elephant armor from this period still exists.*

diverted men from an assault on another English position. But Clive could not have expected that some ten thousand soldiers would now come to lay siege to his few hundred men.

For fifty days a vast army surrounded the crumbling fort, punching holes in its walls and starving the tiny band of defenders, steadily diminishing their numbers. Though it is probably not true, Macaulay reported that the Indian soldiers fighting with Clive were so inspired by his leadership that they made a gallant suggestion: The English, who needed more nourishment, should eat the remaining rice, while the Indians would survive on the water in which it was cooked. No matter how terrible the odds, Clive and his men would not surrender.

The longer the fort held, the more other Indian rulers began to admire Clive and to consider joining in on his side. Word came that thousands of horsemen were on their way to relieve the siege. The attackers tried to bribe Clive, then gave him fair warning: Surrender now or we will kill every man left standing. Macaulay reports that Clive cursed his enemy and told him to think twice before attacking English soldiers.

In one final assault, the Indian leader equipped fighting elephants with steel head plates, so that they could batter down the remaining walls of the fort. But the defenders rained down torrents of concentrated gunfire on the animals. The elephants panicked, turned, and rampaged through their own troops. In an hour of furious battle, Clive lost five or six men—and killed four hundred. The besiegers fled. Once Clive joined up with the relieving troops, he went after his former attacker and destroyed his army.

By pure force of will the twenty-six-year-old Clive had withstood a fifty-day siege, won a complete victory, and changed the balance of power in the region. Clive marched his men to a city named in honor of Dupleix and

In the 1935 film Clive of India, *Loretta Young played Margaret Maskelyne. Margaret's image in the upper-left-hand corner of this poster, where she looms as the inspiration for all of Clive's conquests, does resemble the real woman. In the 1930s Clive was still so well known that a swashbuckling love-story version of his life seemed like a good subject for a feature film.*

obliterated a triumphal column that had been erected to celebrate his victories. Now the English, not the French, were the power on the rise.

Just as English men came to India to seek their fortunes, English women from similar backgrounds traveled east to find proper husbands. Clive's victory suddenly made him an attractive catch, and he found the right woman in Margaret Maskelyne, the sister of one of his good friends. Not long after his great success, Clive returned to Madras and, in a lavish celebration held within Fort St. George, married her. With money, reputation, and a wife, Clive was ready to return to England in glory. But succeeding in English society was a more daunting challenge than fighting ten thousand soldiers.

OUT OF VICTORY, DEFEAT

Upon returning to England, Clive set about to claim his reward. He had already made over 40,000 pounds—which would buy about as much as 6,400,000 modern dollars—in payoffs when working as quartermaster. That astonishing figure gives a sense of how lucrative working in India could be, so long as a person was not very disturbed by qualms about how he earned the money. Not concerned in the slightest about the under-the-table payments, the grateful East India Company offered the hero of Arcot a sword that was inlaid with diamonds and had a golden hilt. Clive refused to accept it until the company agreed to give a similar gift to his mentor, Stringer Lawrence. But neither money nor gifts and praise satisfied him. Clive determined that he should fulfill his father's dream and enter Parliament.

In the eighteenth century Parliament was very proud of itself for having first survived, and then triumphed. Throughout the rest of Europe rulers detested the thought of sharing power with elected officials. Kings and emperors were shutting down ancient legislatures and concentrating power on themselves. In fact, in eastern Europe—the vast lands of what are now Poland, Russia, and the many smaller states near them—the 70 to 80 percent of the people who worked the land were being forced into serfdom. Serfs were virtual slaves, who could be sold with the land and did not have the right to move or change their occupations. In Asia, Africa, and South

America other versions of this same kind of involuntary labor occupied the overwhelming majority of human beings. It is estimated that as late as 1787 three quarters of all the people on the planet performed enforced labor, with only very limited rights.

But in England in the 1600s, when Charles I tried to ignore Parliament and claimed he ruled by God's will, he lost his crown and his head. And in 1689 a new form of government was created that went against this tide of the growing royal power. William of Orange and his wife, Mary, made a deal that gave them the throne in exchange for granting Parliament an inviolable guarantee. For the first time in history, monarchs issued a formal Bill of Rights that not only guaranteed frequent elections and freedom of speech in Parliament but also stated that the royal couple ruled *with* Parliament, that Parliament was necessary to the governance of the nation. This singular compact was part of the events the English happily called The Glorious Revolution. They had a right to be proud: The English had established in law the most inclusive form of any government in the world.

But this marvelous Parliament was a strange institution to be the standard-bearer of democracy. In the eighteenth century Parliament was not meant to express the will of all, most, or even any individual Englishman. In fact, no Catholics could vote or hold office, and even among Englishmen who were eligible to vote, the overwhelming majority had no way to do so.

Parliament has two houses—one only for nobles, called the House of Lords, and one with elected members, called the House of Commons. Members of the House of Commons were elected on the basis of arcane rules, some of which dated back to before the Norman Conquest in 1066, and which Parliament was unwilling to change. This led to some extremely strange and unfair situations. For example, the entire population of Old

Sarum had moved on, leaving "one man, two cows, and a field," but it sent two representatives to the House, as did Dunwich. Dunwich itself, however, did not exist—the site of the former town was now at the bottom of the North Sea.

Locations that had representatives but few or no voters were nicknamed "rotten boroughs," and the local lord who owned the site could handpick the man he wanted for Parliament. Being elected to Parliament in a rotten borough had nothing to do with being popular; it simply meant convincing the right sponsor that you were his man. Money was one very good way to make that argument, as bribing your way into Parliament was a known and accepted practice. Then there were the so-called "pocket boroughs," in which the most powerful person in the area, ranging from a local lord to the king, could strongly influence—and at times even select—the representative he wanted.

While Parliament favored those with power, it completely excluded others. Cities such as Manchester had grown rapidly in recent years—after the last expansion of Parliament. As a result, their tens of thousands of eligible voters enjoyed no representation at all.

England had heroically defended the idea of Parliament, a legislature that could express the will of the nation and check the power of the king. But in practice Parliament was a brokerage house in which influence, alliances, favors, and personalities ruled. As a result, all Clive had to do was to find the right sponsor and the right price, and he could be assured of joining the House of Commons. This he did, allying himself with the Earl of Sandwich, who conveniently controlled a rotten borough in Cornwall and ensured that Clive would get his wish. But Clive did not really understand the game he was playing. His patron was a rather corrupt character who, one persistent

Hogarth made this engraving as part of a series satirizing a particularly corrupt election in 1754. The voter in the center is happily taking bribes from two men at the same time. Hogarth prints are often full of symbols and references to politics and to famous art works, as is this one.

(P199, COURTESY THE BRITISH MUSEUM)

rumor has it, frequented prostitutes and enjoyed participating in sexual dress-up games. Worse, he was allied with the smaller faction in Parliament, and the incoming majority was determined to whittle down its opposition. They questioned Clive's election.

Clive's newfound wealth had raised eyebrows in England. People

John Montagu, the fourth Earl of Sandwich. It is said that placing meat or cheese between slices of bread was named after him, because he wanted food that he could eat easily while he was gambling.

returning from India with new fortunes came to be called "nabobs," a slang version of *nawab,* an Indian title for a regional ruler within the Mogul empire. Nabobs were seen as not entirely trustworthy, or "English." And it is true that under-the-table payments were so common for East India Company employees that they were treated as an expected part of a man's income. But the Parliamentary investigation of Clive's election was not based on his character or his newfound wealth. It wasn't personal at all. Rather, it was that the majority party simply did not want Sandwich's man to take a seat. An investigation by the House cleared Clive. But despite that report, the members voted against him and seated his opponent. This grueling process took up much of the second half of 1754. By the end of the year Clive knew he was beaten, or at least that carrying on the fight would cost more than he could afford. But he had already decided to return to India, where new paths would open to him as a result of the stumbling actions of another man on the rise, who lived in Virginia.

CHAPTER 2

Second Soldier: Into the Forest

THE ARROW

*T*he night is pitch black, rain pours from the sky, and George Washington is leading forty men through the forest in a sneak attack. He is on a mission for England, for his governor, for himself; it is a mission that will go terribly wrong—and change the world.*

The English Civil War that brought Cromwell and his devout Puritans to power also drove people who were loyal to the king overseas. In 1656 John Washington left for Virginia. Washington had lost a good part of his wealth during the conflicts in England, but through careful investment and good connections he once again became land-rich in America.

John's direct descendent George was born in 1732. By then the

Washingtons were well-off. Everything in Virginia was about land. The first English colony in North America, Virginia had a charter that granted it territory all the way to California. No one had any idea what a vast region that was, but anyone with an ounce of ambition felt the lure of those uncharted spaces. As a young man, Thomas Jefferson would have heard his father, Peter, speak of the 800,000 acres, in what would become Kentucky, to which his group of investors in the Loyal Land Company had gained title. When he became president, Jefferson sent two men to lead an expedition to explore and map the west: Meriwether Lewis and William Clark. Lewis's grandfather and Jefferson's father were members of the same company of eager surveyors. So was a man named Thomas Walker, whose explorations took him to a glorious break in the Appalachians he called the Cumberland Gap. Those who surveyed Virginia went on to extend their reach across the continent.

You didn't even have to go into the backwoods to feel the lust for American land. Anyone who had money, and influence in London, did his best to grab what he could. Even before he managed to reclaim the throne of England from the Puritans who had executed his father, Charles II granted a loyal follower a tract of what turned out to be 5 million acres of Virginia. Ironically, the family married the descendents of General Thomas Fairfax, one of the leaders of the rebellion against Charles's father. The Washingtons came to know the Fairfaxes very well.

On their vast estates the squires of Virginia created a kind of life that existed nowhere else on Earth. While English nobles might be as rich, and lived in grander homes, their status depended on their relationship to the king and the court. The Virginia squires were at the top of their world. A squire was expected to be generous and well-read, and yet a man's man who knew the feel of a good tobacco leaf and bred racing horses.

A boy such as George trained to become a squire by spending time with his father—whether watching over the estate or attending a race. Washington grew up to be considered the best horseman in the colony. Unlike Clive, whose father, teachers, and employer all insisted that he fit in, take his place on a well-established path, Washington was encouraged to be self-reliant, to find his own way.

But George was the third son, and just eleven years old when his father died. He was denied his father's example, and his only inheritance was a small, rundown farm. Being close to the wonderful life of the Virginia squires, but a step removed from it, obsessed him. Though the Washingtons were much wealthier than the Clives, George's position was similar to Robert's—near enough to real wealth to know what it could bring, but hobbled by a lack of resources.

Without a father to emulate, Washington diligently copied down 110 rules of behavior from a guidebook called *Rules of Civility and Decent Behavior in Company and Conversation*. The book was originally written in the 1500s by Jesuit priests to instruct French nobility, but it was still read in Washington's day. Some of the rules that he so carefully recorded might have seemed dated even then, such as the firm admonition to "cleanse not your teeth with the tablecloth," or the instruction to avoid killing "fleas, lice, ticks, etc., in the sight of others." The book emphasized respect and deference to social superiors—when walking with an important man, "walk not with him cheek by jowl but somewhat behind him, but yet in such a manner that he may easily speak to you." Washington hoped the *Rules* would make him into a man who would know how to behave around people like the Fairfaxes. This rigid self-discipline was one key to Washington's personality. He was intensely aware of the need to govern himself, and he fashioned his behavior so that he would win honor and respect. He would never allow himself to be lax, casual, or familiar.

Washington's fierce self-control matched his pride in living up to his own high standards. This sounds very different from the familiar image of Americans as casual, easily friendly, even crude, and in some ways it was. But Washington was building himself, managing himself, creating himself with the same care as a hunter learning how to read the animal trails in a forest, a surveyor mapping parcels of land, or a John Winthrop planning a new way of living in a new land. Washington knew that he had the opportunity to better himself, if he could figure out exactly what he must do.

There is something sobering, though, about the fact that the man who truly was the Father of Our Country shaped himself according to ideas of honor and reserve that were so different from what became the American standard. We needed a man who had a very old-fashioned sense of discipline, social distance, and morals to lead us, so that we would have the freedom to invent our own more casual society.

Self-control would give Washington the bearing to comport himself well with important people, but land was the key to wealth. Whether it involved a grand family like the Fairfaxes or a land-speculation firm like the Ohio Company (which had hopes of obtaining 500,000 acres and then selling them off to settlers for a good profit), land was on the minds of all elite men in Virginia. From an early age Washington felt this land hunger. He trained himself as a surveyor so that he could be useful to powerful men and earn enough money to begin buying land himself. He knew that the key to his rise was acquiring what he could, piece by piece, while looking for the main chance, the opportunity to buy some of the cheap but potentially very valuable western lands.

Though painted by Charles Willson Peale in 1772, this portrait of George Washington refers to his earlier life as a young Virginia colonel. He is wearing the uniform of the First Virginia Regiment. The "order of march" in his front pocket and the tents in the background serve to remind viewers of the campaigns he led against the French while wearing that uniform. (Readers interested in this painting can learn more about it in Anderson (see Bibliography), page 738.) (NATIONAL ARCHIVES)

The year that his father died, Washington visited his half brother Lawrence at the impressive estate he had recently named Mount Vernon. In Lawrence, a dashing soldier and an admired, successful man, he saw a living model for the man he wanted to be. At six feet four, George grew up to be very tall for his day. He was fearless, and following in Lawrence's footsteps as a soldier was one way for him to earn the attention and respect of important men. And in 1753, when Washington was just twenty-one, the governor of Virginia asked him to go on a military mission that was crucial to wealthy investors in the Ohio Company. He grabbed the opportunity.

George Washington was a kind of arrow, propelled by his own ambition, the needs of his colony, and of England itself. His target was a French commandant.

Clive fighting against Dupleix and Washington heading off into the wilderness were part of the same global struggle. Both men were simultaneously working for business ventures and for the English military. Commercial and political conflicts overlapped. Just as the French tried to evict the English from India, France had every reason to believe it would dominate North America: It controlled Canada, and through strong Indian alliances it dominated the entire midsection of the continent, running down along the mighty Mississippi to New Orleans. All the French needed to do was to trap the English in their seaboard colonies, and the Protestants would eventually be driven out.

The French were determined to bottle up the English. But leading Virginians were organizing to survey and settle the very land that was the key to French plans. Washington became the fulcrum on which this entire looming conflict rested. He was sent off into the Ohio region to take a message to a suitable French officer, telling him to leave. Of course this would not work, but it was a kind of gauntlet thrown down, a line drawn in the sand. Washington was playing the part of a chivalrous medieval knight: delivering a formal challenge according to rules both he and the French knew and accepted. Washington was not going there to fight but rather to warn that fighting might come soon.

Washington set off on a cold, rainy November day in 1753. As he and his small band of scouts and traders made their way, they had to ford rivers by hanging on to pieces of ice. Leather chaps soon proved better gear than cloth pants. But despite the weather, they were in lush lands: forests that, in other seasons, burst with the colors of maple and cherry trees; fields of rye, clover, and blue grass; and wilderness supporting abundant wildlife. One of the scouts who accompanied Washington had previously reported seeing "turkeys, deer, and elk, and most sorts of game particularly buffaloes." Someone was going to control very valuable land. But who would that be?

THE HALF KING'S GAMBLE

Tanaghrisson—or, as he was called by the English, Half King—was a local Seneca leader in what is now Ambridge, Pennsylvania. In exchange for nearly 1,000 pounds' (160,000 modern dollars') worth of goods, he agreed to let the Virginians build a fortified trading post near present-day Pittsburgh. He intended to pass his newfound wealth along to others, which would reinforce his importance and convince them to join him in siding with the English over the French.

Since Tanaghrisson was allied with the English, he joined Washington's party. But he did not have much influence over the people they met along the way. Instead, it seemed that the French were doing a good job of winning over the Shawnee, Delaware, and Mingo people in the area. And when Washington arrived at a French fort and presented his letter asserting that the territory belonged to the English king, George III, the French commander predictably replied that "the rights of my King, my master, to the lands situated along the Ohio" are "incontestable." Empty proclamations would not decide who was ruler of the Ohio Valley.

After Washington returned to Virginia, the French evicted the English from one key fort and took several prisoners, including a captain named Robert Stobo. Stobo was transferred to Montreal, where he awaited his moment of glory. Virginia's governor sent Washington out again, this time with an undermanned, underpaid detachment of about 160 men, to take the fort back (for a map of Washington's battles with the French, see page 53). The French mustered a small group of perhaps 35 men to, in effect, reverse Washington's previous mission: announce to the English that this was territory belonging to the king of France. This should have been yet another tense but formal exchange; instead, it turned into a massacre.

Washington and his men are marching into the forest. Washington knows that the French are nearby, but where? He first sends about half of his troops in one direction, but then Tanaghrisson arrives with word that he has seen the enemy in the opposite direction. It is now ten at night, and a driving rain is falling. Feeling exposed with half of his men in exactly the wrong place, Washington splits his troops again, leaving forty at the camp. Perhaps a more experienced leader would wait out the night, but Washington is determined to act. He leads the chosen forty through the pitch-black night and pouring rain to reach Tanaghrisson's camp, where they manage to meet up with the now-recovered first party. At sunrise they will attack.

After sneaking single file through the faint dawn light, Washington and Tanaghrisson find the French and surround their camp. The French sense that they are in trouble, for they begin firing, and the English shoot back. The chivalrous exchange is turning into a real battle, and the commander of the French group is down, shot. He asks to parlay with Washington, as is his right. By the very rules of war that protected Washington on his first mission, this should end

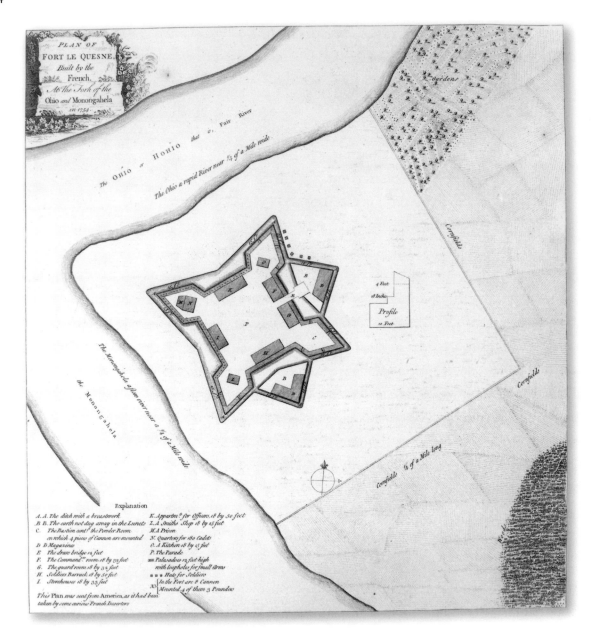

*Robert Stobo made this map of the French Fort Duquesne—the site of modern Pittsburgh—after his capture;
it was smuggled out to the English by Shingas, a Delaware chief.*

(WILLIAM L. CLEMENTS LIBRARY AND THE UNIVERSITY OF MICHIGAN)

the engagement. But Tanaghrisson decides that he cannot accept another incon-
clusive encounter. His standing as a leader of his people depends on the rise of the
English and the destruction of the French. He charges forward and cracks open the
French leader's skull with his hatchet. He then dips his hand into the smashed
head and, according to a soldier's report, "took out his brains and washed his
hands with them."

Washington did not plan for or approve this gruesome murder in the
Ohio forest. A native leader, desperate to show his people that he had chosen the more powerful foreign partner, did that on his own. And none of the
leaders, English, settler, or native, liked the results. Tanaghrisson's action
did nothing to enhance his stature or to convince the Delaware or the
Shawnee to join in the English camp. Instead, he continued to see English
settlers encroaching on the land of his people.

The greed and land hunger of these newcomers were unmistakable. A
New England woman who had been captured when she was a child but
chose to stay and marry an Indian protested to Washington's guide that "she
still remembers they used to be very religious in New England, and wonders
how the white men can be so wicked as she has seen them." A defeated man
who could neither influence his Indian allies nor control his English partners, Tanaghrisson soon died.

In a French counterattack, Washington was overwhelmed and made poor
decisions. On July 4, 1754, he was forced to surrender. He received more
favorable terms for his men than he had expected, but only after he signed a
paper acknowledging that he was responsible for the "assassination" of the
French commander. To make a bad situation worse, the very native nations
Tanaghrisson had hoped to win over led the assault against the English.

Due to their victorious soldiers, and their strong Indian alliances, the

French were the masters of the Ohio Valley, and they had signed proof that the English were treaty breakers. But having lost the peace, the English did have another option, and in London they made plans to begin a decisive war against the French.

Tanaghrisson, the American Indian, gambled that a dramatic show of force would shift the power balance in the Ohio region to his allies. He made the wrong bet. But the bloody murder he committed helped to make a larger war inevitable. Once England and France were no longer jousting in forests and forts but engaged in war, their contest would extend around the globe.

"POOR BRITTONS REMEMBER"

The world war that George Washington inadvertently helped to start began with yet another disaster in which he again played a significant part. Only this time the mistakes in generalship were all on the side of his Scottish superior officer. Even though war between England and France had not yet been formally declared, General Edward Braddock was sent to America to take control of the disputed territory in which Washington had been fighting. Like almost all the English generals, Braddock was contemptuous of the Americans for fighting like Indians. Hiding in the forest, walking single file to evade detection, shooting from behind trees—these were not the tactics

Opposite: *This overhead view shows the column of General Braddock's men at the moment when the French and Indian trap was sprung. The English and Americans march in a carefully laid out geometrical formation, which is useless in the dense woods.*

(WILLIAM L. CLEMENTS LIBRARY AND THE UNIVERSITY OF MICHIGAN)

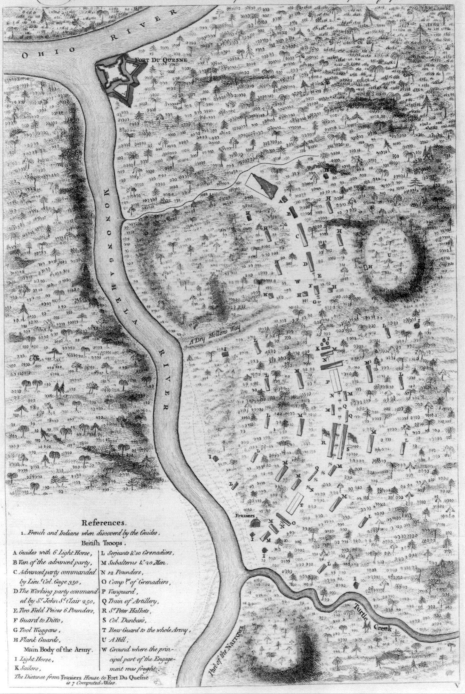

of a great army. Only undisciplined savages fought that way. Real soldiers in the army of the English king stood together, marched proudly, and unflinchingly faced death together. This attitude was reinforced by the rule that any English officer held higher rank than an American, no matter how much experience or authority the American had. To Washington this policy was both an insult and an injustice.

At the head of fourteen hundred English soldiers, and another four hundred led by Washington, Braddock marched off to reclaim the same fort near what is now Pittsburgh that Washington had lost. Led by drummers proudly announcing every step of the march, Braddock's men walked straight into an ambush. Some nine hundred French and Indians, who were perfectly ready to use the cover of the forest to their advantage, devastated Braddock's army, and he was mortally wounded.

Even as one horse after another was shot out from under him, Washington managed to escape, carrying off the dying Braddock with him so he could have a decent burial. A teamster named Daniel Boone was guiding packhorses behind the main force. Seeing the slaughter ahead, he sliced through the harness, mounted a horse, and galloped to safety. He taught his family a sad song about the terrible defeat: "Poor Brittons, poor Brittons, poor Brittons remember/Although we fought hard, we were forced to surrender." Being a good English soldier and being an effective American fighter were turning out to be very different. Did that suggest that Americans were no longer English? Living in the new land, they were becoming something new themselves—part Indian, part European, in time, part African, that is, American.

CHAPTER 3

The Heroes

"THE BLACK HOLE OF CALCUTTA"

The war that began in the Ohio Valley in 1754 was not officially declared until two years later. And by then it was no longer just a fight between England and France over land in North America. Eventually, eleven different European powers, stretching from Russia to Portugal, Sweden to France were drawn into the fighting, and their clashes took place around the globe, from Canada and the Caribbean to Africa, Europe, and Asia. The Seven Years' War, as it came to be called, could just as accurately be titled the First World War.

By the time the full scope of the war became clear, Robert Clive had already returned to Madras to take charge of the East India Company's floundering military campaigns. Word of Braddock's defeat traveled slowly

1. Virginia-Pennsylvania-
   Ohio backcountry,
   1753–55, 1758, 1763–64

2. Minorca, *1756*

3. Central Europe,
   1756–62

4. Plassey, *1757*

5. Senegal, *1758*

6. Quebec, *1759*

7. Martinique and
   Guadeloupe,
   1759, 1761–62

8. Havana, *1762*

9. Manila, *1762*

10. Pontiac's Rebellion,
    1763–65

from the Monongahela River to the Bay of Bengal. But, if anything, events in Bengal upset the English even more.

Located to the northeast, up the coast from Madras, Bengal was the wealthiest, most valuable region in India. Over thousands of years the great Ganges and Brahmaputra ("Son of the Supreme God") rivers have flowed down from the Himalayas to the Bay of Bengal. As the rivers meet the sea, they branch into innumerable paths, forming the largest delta in the world. This vast river-fed landscape was an ideal place for fishing, and for harvesting fruits and vegetables. So long as the seasonal rains appeared on time, it

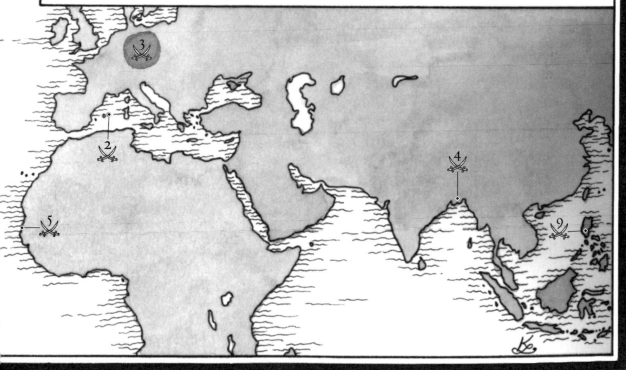

sustained such a lush rice crop that one Dutch visitor called it "the granary of the East."

In 1690 a company employee named Job Charnock founded a trading port where the Hugli, a branch of the Ganges, meets the Bay of Bengal. Calcutta, as it came to be called, was favored with a large, deep, defensible port. With Calcutta as its home base, the company could trade in Bengal's immense stores of grain; in fabric, especially muslin; and in saltpeter—potassium nitrate, which is useful as a fertilizer, as a meat preservative, and as an ingredient in gunpowder. Calcutta, though, was located close enough to salt marshes to be as welcoming a home for disease-bearing mosquitoes as for eager English traders. Calcutta was the richest, and riskiest, post for a company employee.

When Clive returned to India, the new ruler of Bengal was a man named Siraj Ud-Daula. Like Tanaghrisson, he was increasingly pressed to choose which of two dangerous European powers he would make his ally. Like the American Indian, the Bengali Indian knew that the Europeans were building or reinforcing forts so that they could fight each other on his territory. For the moment, he chose to side with the French. On June 26, 1756, he drove the English out of Calcutta.

When he took the city, perhaps as many as 146 of the captured European men and women were herded into a tiny cell with hardly any air. In one horrifying night an estimated 123 of them died, including a man named Patrick Johnstone. Macaulay wrote of the "Black Hole of Calcutta": "Nothing in history or fiction . . . approaches the horrors which were recounted by the few survivors of that night. They cried for mercy. They strove to burst the door . . . then the prisoners went mad with despair. They trampled each other down, fought for places at the windows, fought for the pittance of water with which the cruel mercy of the murderers mocked their agonies, raved, prayed, blasphemed, implored the guards to fire among them. The gaolers [jailers] in the meantime held lights to bars, and shouted with laughter at the frantic struggles of their victims." Though in fact he neither knew of nor ordered the detention, for generations afterward Siraj stood as the vivid symbol of oriental cruelty.

Macaulay based his vivid descriptions on the only account of the horrifying night, which was written by an English survivor named John Z. Holwell. Holwell was eager to highlight the Indians' cruelty and exaggerated every-

The courthouse and "writers' building" in eighteenth-century Calcutta, as painted by Thomas Daniell. Clive started out as a "writer"—a low-level clerk. The large building gives a sense of the power of the English, while the street shows many Indians. Paintings of India and other parts of Asia and the Middle East by Thomas Daniell and his brother William were very much like the travel magazines and TV shows we have today. They offered customers in England a carefully shaped visual introduction to the East. (P 95, COURTESY THE BRITISH LIBRARY)

thing, including the count of those crammed into the cell. On the other hand, even Siraj's supporters reported that he had a cruel streak. And whatever his personality, he was a weak leader who made poor choices in a difficult situation. Although the incident the English focused on was distorted, they picked the right enemy.

Clive did not know about the deaths in the infamous "Black Hole," but he was determined to retake the city and to deliver a crushing blow to the French. By January 1757 he had recaptured Calcutta, and in June he was ready to take on the nawab's army directly. He had just one problem: He commanded only three thousand men, while Siraj could put fifty thousand soldiers into the field. Nevertheless, Clive marched ahead, until he reached the last river he would have to cross before starting to fight. There he stopped. Poised at the banks of the Hugli, he had to decide: Was crossing it brave or suicidal? For the first and only time in his short but stellar military career, Clive held council with his senior staff, then went off to be by himself and think.

The next two hundred years of English and Indian history may have been determined while Clive sat beside the river and weighed his alternatives. For when he finally decided to lead his men into battle, Clive gave the East India Company an empire.

Soon after the armies met at Plassey (now Palashi) on June 23, rain began to fall. Clive's men were standing in mud in front of a grove of mango trees that extended beyond sight—it was known as Laksha Bagh, the Orchard of a Hundred Thousand Trees. They faced an immense army including elephants "covered with scarlet cloth and embroidery; their horse [men] with their drawn swords glittering in the sun; their heavy cannon drawn by vast trains of oxen; and their standards flying." Clive erected tents to cover his big guns, while his enemy failed to protect his powder, which was soon useless. This was just one reason why the vastly superior forces of the Bengali ruler were utterly routed by Clive and his men—one of whom was Patrick Johnstone's brother John. There was also the fact that many men simply did not fight: Their leaders had been bribed—or convinced—not to fight for a ruler they disliked.

The legend spells out the key moments of the Battle of Plassey. Even at a glance, the difference in size between Clive's small army pressed against two sides of the mango grove and Siraj's legions is unmistakable. Cassembuzzer was the name the English used for a river now called the Bhagirathi. The Bhagirathi joins with the Julangi near Plassey (now Palashi) to form the Hugli, though many maps refer to the entire river system as the Hugli. Since India became independent, Plassey is no longer considered worth remembering. The entirely neglected site has a single memorial pillar, and a recent visitor reported that it was being well employed—a local farmer used it to tether a goat.

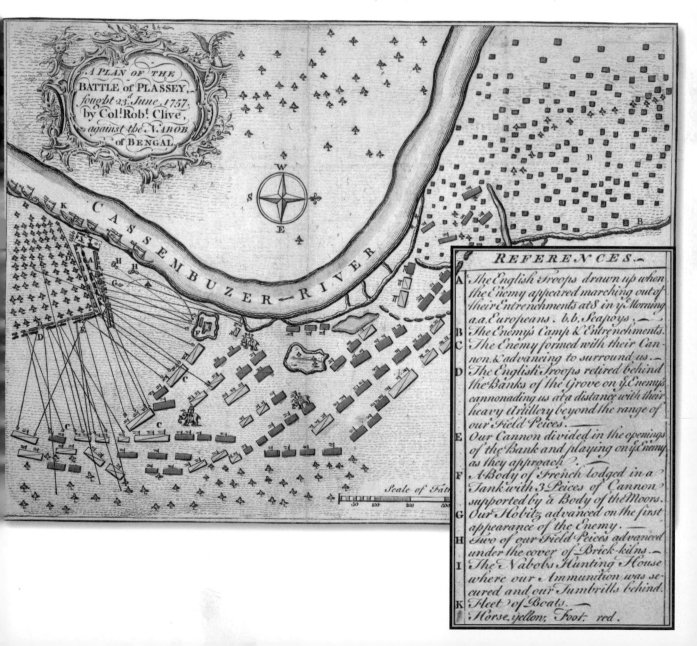

A PLAN OF THE
BATTLE of PLASSEY,
fought 23.d June, 1757,
by Col.l Rob.t Clive,
against the NABOB
of BENGAL.

CASSEMBUZER RIVER

Scale of Fath.

REFERENCES.

A The English Troops drawn up when the Enemy appeared marching out of their Entrenchments at 8 in y.e Morning a.a. Europeans. b.b. Seapoys.
B The Enemy's Camp & Entrenchments.
C The Enemy formed with their Cannon, & advancing to surround us.
D The English Troops retired behind the Banks of the Grove on y.e Enemys cannonading us at a distance with their heavy Artillery beyond the range of our Field Peices.
E Our Cannon divided in the openings of the Bank and playing on y.e Enemy as they approach.
F A Body of French lodged in a Tank with 3 Peices of Cannon supported by a Body of the Moors.
G Our Hobitz advanced on the first appearance of the Enemy.
H Two of our Field Peices advanced under the cover of Brick-kilns.
I The Nabobs Hunting House where our Ammunition was secured and our Tumbrills behind.
K Fleet of Boats.
   Horse, yellow; Foot, red.

This painting shows Clive meeting Mir Jafar just after the battle of Plassey. Mir Jafar is on the right of this painting, bowing slightly to Clive. The barely bridled horse near Clive contrasts with the massive, still elephant near Mir Jafar. The artist wants viewers to see Clive as European and energetic, Mir Jafar as Asian and passive. (NPG, Courtesy the National Portrait Gallery, London)

All spring Clive had been conspiring with wealthy Indian merchants who detested and mistrusted Siraj. Mir Jafar, a great-uncle by marriage of Siraj's who led a good number of the men in the nawab's army, was part of the plot, for he was to be installed as the new nawab with the endorsement of the victorious British. One important merchant, named Omichand, though, demanded a particularly high payoff to be the secret go-between, ferrying messages between Clive and Mir Jafar. Clive answered this plot with one of his own. He wrote up a fake treaty with a forged signature from a British admiral that accepted Omichand's terms. He hid the real agreement, which gave him no reward at all. This was just one way in which he was willing to bend, alter, or completely ignore the rules of business and politics—at least as those rules were discussed in public.

Any doubts raised in England by Braddock's defeat in America were completely erased by Clive's triumph in India. Not only had he, again, overcome seemingly impossible odds and crushed a ruler allied with the French, he had made the East India Company into the dominant power in a region legendary for its wealth. With warriors like Clive, it seemed that England could master its enemies anywhere in the world. But what kind of a man was he? Even as Clive triumphed in battle, his enemies in England attacked him: He did everything his own way, he made up the rules as he went along, he would not accept discipline. Clive, you might say, was as independent as the American colonists, and that was very dangerous, indeed.

THE THIRD AND PERFECT SOLDIER: JAMES WOLFE

By 1759 the English campaign in North America had recovered from Braddock's defeat. The year before, General John Forbes had slowly and carefully carved a new wagon road through the forest. Then, assisted by George Washington, now commander of the Virginia military, Forbes forced the French to abandon and burn the fort Braddock had died trying to win. Now just one impregnable city stood between the English and success in North America: Quebec. If the English could conquer the city and take Canada, they would not only ensure their domination of North America but deliver a decisive blow to the French. A contest for one city was a crucial pivot in the war for power and influence throughout the world.

Raised above surrounding rivers by steep cliffs and protected by 16,000 French, Canadian, and Indian fighters, the city posed an impossible challenge for attackers. There were precious few pathways up from the St. Lawrence River, and the French guarded them. As the French commander, the Marquis Louis-Joseph de Montcalm, wrote, "We need not suppose that the enemy have wings."

But Robert Stobo, the English captain who had been captured in the Ohio Valley and sent to Montreal, had made very good use of his time in the north. He had gained the confidence of his captors and was allowed freedom of the city. Treated as an appealing guest, he was actually making careful observations and drawing secret maps. When Braddock was killed, the French captured his baggage, including a map that Stobo had, foolishly, signed. Suddenly, he was no longer cordial and charming, he was a spy, and was sentenced to death. But in May 1759 he escaped, carrying with him new maps—and a great secret. Stobo had discovered a pathway up from the St. Lawrence to Quebec that the French ignored. A force landing at Fuller's Cove could snake its way up the cliffs and arrive untouched at the Plains of Abraham a few miles west of the city.

In July, Stobo sailed back toward the city of his captivity along with an English force under the leadership of Major General James Wolfe. Armed with Stobo's knowledge, Wolfe dared to attempt the impossible. The final battle did not take place until September 13. By that time, the English had exhausted all alternatives, and they knew that if this last assault failed, they would have to depart for the winter. Wolfe was in poor health and might not be able to return. This was his moment.

On a moonless night lit only by stars, Wolfe began to murmur in a low voice to the officers near him in one of the lead boats. He was reciting a poem by Thomas Gray, a poem about death. What might those soldiers have felt? They were on a dangerous mission in the Canadian night, and their frail, sickly leader was speaking reverently about dying. "The paths of glory lead but to the grave," he intoned. Then, after finishing the last words—about a gravestone in a churchyard—he added that "I would rather have written those lines than take Quebec."

Once upon a time, historians saw in Wolfe's recital a sign of true greatness. As the nineteenth-century historian Francis Parkman commented just after quoting Wolfe's lines, "None were there to tell him that the hero is greater than the poet." But a recent student of this war thinks Wolfe was driven by his own compulsions to seek a heroic death in battle, and was completely callous about risking the lives of all his men to accomplish that end. How reassuring was it to know that your leader was expecting to die? Whether he was a hero or a madman, Wolfe's complete lack of fear allowed him to take senseless risks. Led by Major Isaac Barré, Wolfe's men stormed up Stobo's path to win a great victory—or to perish.

When Montcalm was awakened to see a long, thin line of perhaps 4,500 red-coated soldiers standing where they could not possibly be, he had a terrible sense of doom. Even more disheartening was the discipline of the soldiers. They stood unflinching as Canadian and Indian snipers shot at them from nearby woods. When cannon fire threatened his men, Wolfe did something even more daring: He ordered them to lie down on the field of battle so they would be more difficult targets, while he paced and pranced in front of them, taunting the French and drawing their fire. The soldiers' courage and discipline, their absolute obedience, the officers' unflinching determination—all the virtues the English treasured in their fighting men shone forth that day on the Plains of Abraham.

At least that is what later Englishmen believed. Wolfe can just as easily be seen as half crazed and reckless. He had no plan once his men reached the field of battle. And if Montcalm had simply held his fire until the reinforcements he knew were on the way arrived and attacked the English from behind, Wolfe's men would have been slaughtered. Instead, he panicked and led his men straight into battle. French soldiers marched, as they were

Benjamin West's dramatic painting The Death of General Wolfe *was first shown in London in 1771, where it created a sensation. Even this later engraved version by William Woolett sold thousands of copies. West was the first to paint events from recent history on such a grand scale, which showed that he considered Wolfe to be a modern hero, and the battle for empire a story for the ages. This scene is a fictionalized reconstruction, not an attempt to record exactly what took place on the Plains of Abraham.*
(LIBRARY OF CONGRESS)

trained, directly forward at the English guns. But the Canadian militia broke ranks and ran ahead, each man charging on his own surge of battle fever.

The double row of English, calm and silent, waited, and waited. They were to hold their fire until the enemy was just forty yards away. But at three times that distance the French soldiers stopped, dropped down to one knee, and began to fire. Wolfe was hit, his wrist shattered. Though in excruciating pain, he simply wrapped the splintered bones with a handkerchief and carried on. As the French and Canadians approached, they were met by the English fighting like a giant mechanical battery of guns: wait, sight the enemy, fire, kneel, reload, fire. The machine mowed down anyone who neared it; the terrified French broke ranks and fled. In the pursuit Wolfe was shot and killed; Barré took a shot in the head; Montcalm was mortally wounded and died the next day. On September 18, five days after Wolfe's men climbed the footpath, Quebec formally surrendered.

In the early 1760s the view from London should have been most pleasant. After the triumphs of Wolfe and Clive, victory in the global war was at hand. Yet reports coming from both east and west were disturbing. When Clive returned home in 1760, he was worth at least 270,000 pounds, or 43,200,000 modern dollars, making him one of the richest men in England. And as a reward for installing him as the new nawab, Mir Jafar granted Clive a title that came with an annual payment of another 27,000 pounds. This sort of gift was not unusual in India at the time—Clive's French rival Dupleix, for one, had received similar payments. But Mir Jafar had been exceptionally clever. The honor he gave Clive was to be paid for by taxes from land the company already controlled. So while the Indian ruler was generous in spirit, it was the East India Company that would have to pay the bills. Clive

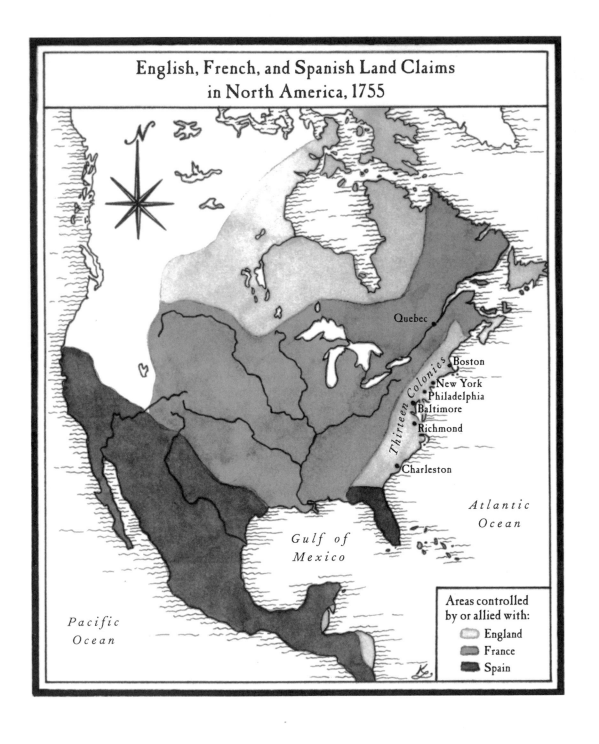

English, French, and Spanish Land Claims
in North America, 1755

Quebec

Boston

New York
Philadelphia
Baltimore
Richmond

Thirteen Colonies

Charleston

Atlantic Ocean

Gulf of Mexico

Pacific Ocean

Areas controlled
by or allied with:

England

France

Spain

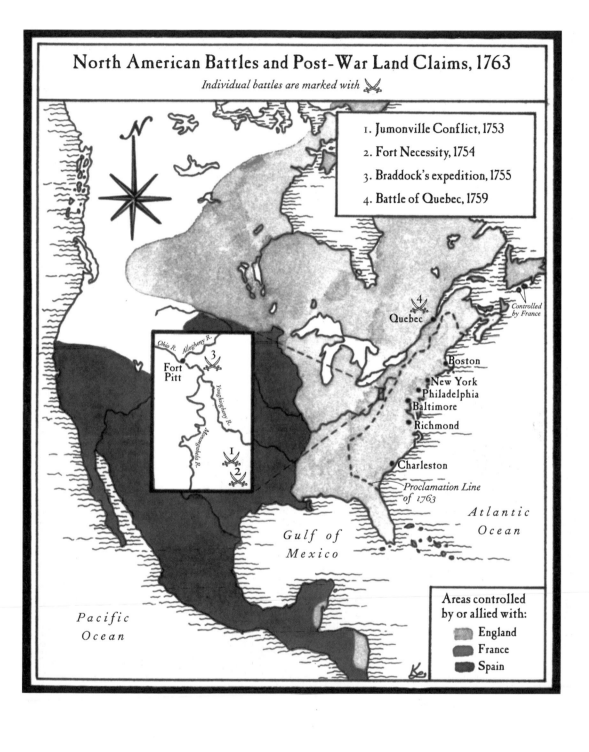

North American Battles and Post-War Land Claims, 1763

Individual battles are marked with ⚔

1. Jumonville Conflict, 1753
2. Fort Necessity, 1754
3. Braddock's expedition, 1755
4. Battle of Quebec, 1759

N

4
Quebec

Controlled by France

Boston
New York
Philadelphia
Baltimore
Richmond

Charleston

Proclamation Line of 1763

Ohio R.   *Allegheny R.*
Fort Pitt
3

Youghiogheny R.

Monongahela R.

1
2

Atlantic Ocean

Gulf of Mexico

Pacific Ocean

Areas controlled by or allied with:

England
France
Spain

Major General Jeffrey Amherst's sense of superiority seems evident in this engraving based on a portrait by Sir Joshua Reynolds. Amherst did not actually wear armor in battle—Reynolds chose that costume to honor him as a victorious knight. Reynolds was a leading English painter and president of the Royal Academy; he and Hogarth completely disagreed on the nature of art. (LIBRARY OF CONGRESS)

had turned himself into a kind of prince, and had made a trading company into a foreign landlord. This was simply not done. The news from North America was no better. Major General Jeffrey Amherst, the British army officer who had overseen Wolfe's campaign, described the colonials as lazy, selfish thieves utterly without discipline or character. Overseas English, it seemed, forgot the rules of true civilization that they had learned at home.

Washington's losses in the Ohio Valley brought the English to the brink of world war. Wolfe's impossible triumph and heroic death swept them to victory. Clive's superhuman bravado extended England's reach deep into Asia. Yet precisely these successes led directly to new and interconnected emergencies in North America, in India, and in England itself. One part of that global crisis is called the American Revolution.

RIGHTS
AND
RULES

CHAPTER 4

Three Challenges

THE LEGAL CHALLENGE: A CHILD IS BORN IN BOSTON

Managing an empire that now stretched around the world, from land-hungry colonists in North America to equally rapacious merchants in India, was especially challenging to London because no one really understood how such a vast enterprise should work. The so-called "dismal science" of economics had not been invented yet, and an ever-changing set of philosophers, bankers, and government ministers struggled to make sense of the newly interconnected worlds. The one model England had was Spain, which had conquered the wealthy Aztec and Inca kingdoms and then stripped them of as much gold and silver as could be shipped across the Atlantic. The mother country sent out soldiers, governors, and priests and was paid back in precious ores.

Based on the Spaniards' experience, theoreticians came up with a plan for trade and empire that came to be called "mercantilism." The essence of the plan was that gold should flow in one direction only: from distant ports and settlements back to the center of the empire. Of course the colonies would need to develop some business and trade of their own, but their entire purpose was to serve the homeland—which in turn offered them protection, and membership in a world empire. In effect, the colonies were like the modern franchise restaurants and coffee shops that can be found on every street corner and in every mall. To be able to use the company logo (the flag of England) and sell its products, they had to keep sending gold back to headquarters. No one today would expect a local Starbucks, for example, to declare itself independent of the chain, which is exactly how London viewed its colonies.

Mercantilism looked better on paper than it did in North America or in India. In fact, the overseas English needed their own supplies of gold and silver to do business, and they could not keep feeding the homeland. Still, London insisted that the Spanish model should apply—wealth created around the world must be directed back to the center, to England. That was fine in theory but nearly meaningless in practice.

New England is gifted with a long coastline filled with bays, rivers, coves, and jetties, which enabled its merchants to become excellent smugglers. And if anything, the New York traders, who could make deals with Indians inland and offload mysterious cargoes from ships at the shoreline, were even more accomplished at making up their own rules of trade. From the point of view of London and its officials in America, this was an outrage. During the war, even as great men such as Wolfe made the ultimate sacrifice, these unprincipled, selfish children traded with the enemy. When an officer of the law noticed, he was bribed or intimidated into silence.

There was, however, another way to view the connections among corruption, smuggling, and the law. Colonial merchants saw conspiracy everywhere: West Indian plantation owners grown immensely wealthy from the sugar cane planted and picked by their endless legions of slaves often lived in London. There they could twist the minds of officials, setting up terms of trade that punished North American shippers. If, in order to stay in business, a merchant had to pick up some molasses from a French island, that was not disloyalty—it was a matter of survival. Grand theories about how colonies should support the motherland meant nothing if they drove merchants and traders into bankruptcy. And what of the officials whom London sent to the colonies?

In 1761 Francis Bernard, the governor of New Jersey, was shifted to the same post in Massachusetts. His only qualification for office was that he had married the cousin of Lord Barrington, the king's secretary of war. Always scrambling to make money to support his ten children, Bernard was glad to get the new job because it brought a higher salary. Every decision he made seemed linked to money. When he had to appoint a new chief justice of the Massachusetts Supreme Court, he snubbed the senior James Otis, a trained lawyer who had been promised the job by a previous governor. Otis's son, also named James, held a government post, but was not at all vigilant in prosecuting smugglers. As governor, Bernard would get to keep one third of any smuggled cargo that was confiscated. Rather than take an Otis, he picked Thomas Hutchinson.

A direct descendent of Anne Hutchinson, the forceful woman who had clashed with John Winthrop and the Puritan leaders of her day, Thomas had none of her passionate spirit. Nor did he have any legal training. What he did have was a healthy respect for traditional authority and an ever-growing network of family connections with powerful people.

To the heirs of the Puritans, who still made up a significant part of the population of Massachusetts, some seriously troubling things were happening: Offices were for sale, or available if you toadied to the right official. The kind of prostitution that made London a hive of evil was crossing the water. Government was sliding away from good men into the hands of corrupt officials who wielded secret power.

Bernard took office in 1760, the same year the new king, George III, ascended to the throne. One of the best tools he could use against smugglers—which would also bring him some nice dividends when their illegal cargoes were divided up—was a legal paper called a "writ of assistance." This document allowed officials to enter a warehouse or even a private home if they so much as suspected that it contained smuggled goods. These writs were commonly granted in England and had been used in Massachusetts in the past. But by law they had to be renewed by each new king. Several merchants who had been caught now found a young Boston lawyer who was willing to question the legality of the writs—James Otis Jr.

What a perfect catastrophe in the making: on one side, the new governor and the new chief justice upholding the law as it was written and practiced. On the other, an eloquent man inspired to brilliance by anger over his father's treatment. In this shattering collision, the American Revolution began. For when the merchants were brought to court, Otis did not debate the facts of the case. Instead, he raised a much larger and more troubling issue: No matter what the law said, it was not valid if it was not just. The English Parliament did not have the right to rule the colonies in any way it saw fit, but only in a fashion that was fair. As Otis would put it later, "The Parliament cannot make 2 and 2, 5."

Otis had spoken the unmentionable: The colonies were not children

James Otis Jr. Here Otis is surrounded by Hercules and Minerva, who is carrying a "liberty cap." Look at this again after you have seen the image of John Wilkes on page 134.

needing regulation and guidance by their wiser parent. They were equals, with the full rights of Englishmen. And as equals, they were as likely to judge as to be judged. What the English called selfishness was healthy self-interest. They were, in a word, independent.

Another lawyer, named John Adams, was part of the large crowd in the courthouse, and years later he recorded what he had seen: "Near the fire were seated five judges, with Lieutenant Governor Hutchinson at their head as chief justice, all in their new fresh robes of scarlet English cloth, in their broad bands, and immense judicial wigs [and against them James Otis,] a flame of fire! . . . Then and there the child Independence was born."

THE MILITARY CHALLENGE: REBELLION IN THE APPALACHIAN FOOTHILLS

James Otis spoke with passion and articulated important ideas, but the challenge he presented to English rule was a lawyer's debate, heard in a courtroom. London faced more violent threats on the western borders of the colonies. The victory of the English in the long war was disastrous to Indians who had been allied with the French. Suddenly, relationships with French traders and soldiers that had protected Indian lands, and had offered them a powerful partner, were useless. Worse yet, Major General Amherst decided that it was time to put a complete stop to diplomacy American style—no more gifts to win the favor and allegiance of Indian leaders. English discipline had won the war, and it was time for English rules to govern America. Indian nations were squeezed between the rigidity of the new conqueror and the constant invasions of settlers with rifles. The only people eager to appease them were land speculators, offering plenty of liquor and gifts in exchange for signatures on deeds—each of which carved off another huge chunk of Indian land.

In 1762, though, a new path opened. The old gods had seen the Indians' need and sent them a prophet: Neolin, the Enlightened One, appeared at a town called Tuscarawas on the Muskingum River (near modern Bolivar, Ohio). Though the settlement consisted of perhaps forty huts, it was an important gathering place for the Delaware. And Neolin was a Delaware who had been granted an astonishing vision. Neolin had once given in to the temptations of alcohol. But by following a woman clad in white to the land of the spirits, he learned the plan that the Master of Life had for native peoples. They must turn away completely from the ways of the whites and return to their traditional practices. To make fire, they should only rub sticks together. For seven years all would be purified; the young warriors must hunt and fight only with bows and arrows, and women and older people should eat corn. After seven years they would return to wearing skins, and live as their ancestors once had. The Indians must rid themselves of the influences of the outsiders and "drive off your land those dogs clothed in red who will do you nothing but harm."

Neolin's message brought hope to many Indians. It told them to find strength and power by returning to older ways. But as he traveled from one group to another spreading his vision and selling special diagrams mapping out the relationship of Indians, whites, and the Master of Life, Neolin also inspired Indians to take up arms and fight. By the summer of 1763, nations across the Great Lakes region and down through the Ohio Valley were coordinating attacks on English forts such as Detroit, Pitt (now Pittsburgh), and Niagara.

The Ottawa chief who led the assault on Detroit was named Pontiac, and so this uprising is known as Pontiac's Rebellion. The English were both frightened and infuriated by the clever, widespread attacks. The Indians showed no mercy, killing as many as two thousand settlers in their effort to remove the English from their lands. In turn, a colonel, who was trying to organize a relief column for Fort Pitt, described the Indians as "vermin" whom he hoped to exterminate. Acting on the same idea, Colonel Simeon Ecuyer helped to end the siege of the fort by giving the Delaware blankets taken from a smallpox hospital. Major General Amherst, who had been so disdainful of his American soldiers, supported both the drive to kill all of the Indians and the practice of using smallpox blankets to spread disease.

Is there a villain in this combat? The Indians and the English were equally willing to kill civilians and use terror as a weapon—it is no more accurate to blame the English for using germ warfare in the hope of exterminating the Indians than to single out the Indians for being as cruel as they could be to scare off their enemies. But even that is sobering. Both sides behaved savagely, and this has been a constant theme of American history— at the edges and frontiers where people desperate to hold on to their lands are pitted against others equally determined to build new lives, barbarism rules.

Amherst stalled on reporting the uprising. English officials simply could not imagine that American Indians were defeating their proud troops, and the more successful Pontiac was, the angrier they were at their general. Pontiac's Rebellion failed because the Indians ran out of ammunition and so could not sustain their assaults on well-defended forts. But the Indians had given the English a scare, and Amherst was relieved of his command. If the English wanted to avoid new conflicts, new bloodshed, new expenses, they would have to offer some security to the besieged native peoples, who had already lost their land along the eastern coast and now lived to the west of the Alleghenies.

* * *

THE MOB'S CHALLENGE: HELLFIRE IN LONDON

The Earl of Sandwich may have been able to indulge his taste for sex mixed with weird ceremonies because he was one of the so-called Monks of St. Francis of Wycomb. If one account is to be believed, this was not a religious order; instead, it was a group of twelve men who had converted a former abbey into what became known as the Hell-Fire Club. As the name suggests, this was a place in which the "monks" could meet prostitutes, or even noble ladies with a yen for sexual adventure, and mock the normal rules of religion and marriage. One day at the club the earl met a member of Parliament from London named John Wilkes, who was known equally for his radical views and his pursuit of women. Sandwich joked that Wilkes was sure to die either on the scaffold or of venereal disease. Wilkes replied, "That depends, My Lord, whether I embrace your mistress or your principles."

Wilkes was the kind of compelling bad boy who is always going one step too far—and is all the more charismatic for doing it. Like Clive, he bought his way into Parliament, spending 7,000 pounds (1,120,000 modern dollars) to purchase the votes he needed. But his real power was not as a legislator. As the Seven Years' War neared its end, Wilkes found a new way to provoke and challenge. In his newspaper, *The North Briton,* he implied that a Scotsman named John Stuart, the Earl of Bute, who was the king's former tutor and now favorite minister, was having an affair with the king's mother. Wilkes's mockery, his take-no-prisoners style, his irreverence toward authority, made him popular with London's endless legions of struggling workingmen and -women as well as its desperately poor. He spoke for them, and they loved their champion. And then he crossed a sacred line, for in issue number 45 of *The North Briton,* he implied that the king himself had lied to Parliament. Wilkes was at once arrested.

By English law a member of Parliament could be jailed only for certain very serious crimes—which did not include insulting the king. The lord chief justice himself set Wilkes free. The waiting crowd chanted, "Liberty! Liberty! Wilkes Forever!" Now all the forces of the king and his allies turned on Wilkes. Trying one court action after another, they managed to remove him from his seat in Parliament. And, in 1764, he fled to Paris.

For the moment, Wilkes was out of power and away from England. But the surging crowd that saw him as their hero filled London's streets, and their cause was something they called "liberty"—freedom of the press, freedom from oppression, yes. But "Wilkes and Liberty" was also a howling demand for attention from people who lived short and very hard lives. No one had spoken for them since the defeat of the Levellers and other radicals during the English Civil War. In 1647 the Levellers tried, but failed, to convince Oliver Cromwell that England should become a real democracy, and after his death even that voice of protest was silenced. London's mobs recognized in Wilkes's impertinence someone who saw life the same way they did.

As Parliament met to deal with the aftermath of the Seven Years' War, the members knew that just outside their doors were masses of people who had been inspired by a dangerous man and by even more dangerous passions and ideas.

Opposite: *Hogarth's comment on the tensions of the moment appears on page 69, and that image includes a slight satire of John Wilkes. Wilkes attacked Hogarth for this in his paper,* The North Briton. *Hogarth replied with this sketch, drawing a cross-eyed, devilish Wilkes. But Wilkes's many supporters liked Hogarth's satire, for it echoed their angry chant, "Wilkes and Liberty."* The North Briton *45 was the most controversial issue of the paper, and from then on, anytime a drawing included the number, it was referring to Wilkes—see, for example, page 96. The "liberty cap" is the same as the one carried by Minerva in the portrait of James Otis Jr. on page 61.*

(BM SAT 4050, COURTESY THE BRITISH MUSEUM)

CHAPTER 5

London Responds

The Prime Minister

George Grenville became prime minister, the head of England's government, in 1763, just as his nation signed the Treaty of Paris, ending the long war with France. The path ahead of him was absolutely clear. Winning a world war is expensive. England's national debt nearly doubled during the war to 129 million pounds, or almost 21 billion modern dollars, and just the interest on the debt was gobbling up another 4.5 million pounds (720 million dollars) a year. But people in England would not stand for any new taxes—they were already the most heavily taxed people in Europe, and angry protests against specific taxes had begun. If Grenville could not ask the English to pay more, it was obvious who were not pulling their weight: the North American colonists. One historian has estimated that taxpayers in

Hogarth favored Grenville's plan to sign a treaty with France and end the Seven Years' War. In this print, "The Times," he gives a sense of the tensions of the moment. The crouching fireman in the center is the king, trying to put out many flames on the globe; Lord Bute was Scottish, and here Scots are good firemen helping out. John Wilkes is one of the faceless men high up in the windows of the building in the center, shooting water at the king—not helping, but making trouble.

(P211(I), COURTESY THE BRITISH MUSEUM)

England paid twenty-six times as much to the government as those in Massachusetts, Pennsylvania, or Maryland, and those fortunate enough to live in New York and Virginia paid even less.

Americans were also supposed to pay an extra charge for many products

Lord Clive, Baron of Plassey, in a print that may have been based on a painting by Gainsborough.
(P791, COURTESY THE BRITISH LIBRARY)

purchased overseas and shipped into the colonies. But they were such accomplished smugglers, and the English officials who were supposed to check on them were so weak and so corrupt, that England collected the ridiculous amount of just 1,800 pounds (288,000 dollars) a year from these charges.

Facing a rebellion by American Indians inspired by a prophet, a crushing debt, and North American colonists who had not served well in war and had it all too easy in peace, Grenville knew exactly what to do. He would create order and rationality in the empire. First, he would forbid the Americans from crossing the Alleghenies into Indian territory, establishing a

Proclamation Line beyond which land was reserved for the Indians. That would diminish the provocations that alarmed the Indians and that cost English tax dollars to resolve. Second, he would leave 10,000 soldiers in America to maintain the peace, discourage the French, and encourage the colonists to listen to reason. Third, he would tighten up on customs inspectors—who would take their work seriously or lose their jobs. Fourth, he would pay for the army and for new courts to hear customs cases by changing the rules so that the colonists would actually have to pay the duties or taxes they owed. He would lower the tax on molasses so that there was no advantage to smuggling it, but he would make damn sure every American ship carrying the rich dark liquid paid what it owed. And he indicated that when he had worked out the details, he would create a new "stamp tax"—a charge on every piece of paper used as an official document. From London's point of view, Grenville's plan was clear, reasonable, and intelligent.

THE EAST INDIA COMPANY

In his usual cycle of exertion and collapse, Clive's health gave out in India after his great triumph. But on his return to London he proceeded to claim his rightful place in English society. He found a district where he could run for Parliament with no opposing candidate—and another equally easy spot for his father. He was made a lord, a baron, but only of an estate in Ireland, which meant he would not automatically sit in the House of Lords. This was a snub, but Clive knew how to deal with small-minded opponents: He renamed his estate Plassey, so he would be known as Lord Plassey—which would remind everyone of his spectacular triumph whenever they spoke his

This meeting room at the headquarters of the East India Company was the scene of many of Clive's battles with Sulivan and the Johnstones. (WD2465, COURTESY THE BRITISH LIBRARY)

name. Yet there was one challenge to his power that he could not so easily dismiss: The director of the East India Company was a poor Irishman named Laurence Sulivan who had risen to his high post through extreme diligence and brilliant calculation. Sulivan was as much an outsider as was Clive, but he decided to throw all his considerable skill into curbing Clive's power. He started by proposing that the company not pay the special annual payment Clive was slated to receive.

In 1763, even as Grenville was working out the details of his new rules and regulations, Clive and Sulivan went to war against each other. They were perfect adversaries: Clive, the bold soldier who would never doubt himself and never retreat; Sulivan, the clever tactician who was absolutely devoted to control and power. This was not a military campaign but rather a contest of stockholders for control of the richest, most powerful company in England. Whoever controlled the most shares would win.

One large block of shares was controlled by a set of ambitious Scottish brothers who have left their traces on the history of three continents. George Johnstone lived such an action-packed life, you would think he was a character in a novel—he actually took part in scenes involving ships sailing in disguise to get close to the enemy that were exactly like those filmed in *Master and Commander*. The hotheaded younger son of a Scottish lord, he managed to get aboard a navy ship in his early teens. His "rash bravery" drew attention when, in full sight of enemy guns, he clambered on board a burning ship and attached a chain to it, so it could be pulled out of harm's way. He was equally determined in clashing with his superior officers when he did not get the credit he thought he deserved. Still, his wild courage in battle, and connections back home, allowed Johnstone to rise through the ranks of the navy. Then he got his big chance.

After the Seven Years' War, the English gained control of what was called West Florida (a sliver of land along the Gulf of Mexico running from the Apalachicola River in what is now Florida to the Mississippi), and, through the influence of Lord Bute, his fellow Scotsman, Johnstone was appointed governor. But he delayed leaving for this plum assignment. While one of his brothers, Patrick, had died in the "Black Hole," another brother, John, who had fought beside Clive at Plassey, was in Calcutta. John was employed by the East India Company, and he used his position to intimidate Indian rulers and extort huge bribes and personal payoffs. Some in the com-

George Johnstone does not look like the daring young naval fighter in this later portrait, but if you look at page 113, you can see the family resemblance to his brother John.

(BHC2808, NATIONAL MARITIME MUSEUM, LONDON)

pany were starting to object, and George saw an opportunity in the fight between Clive and Sulivan—he would swing the considerable power of the Johnstone family and its ill-gotten fortune behind whoever would guarantee that his brother and his money were safe.

At first George Johnstone leaned toward Clive. But Clive would not quiet his objections to John's truly obnoxious, greedy, and destructive behavior, even for the votes he needed, while Sulivan happily made that bargain. Sulivan found other partners on the highest levels of government, and with the Johnstones on his side, he won the first round of his titanic battle to control the company. The stockholders ruled against Clive, and at the end of 1763 he lost his annual payment.

Clive was not the type of warrior who could accept defeat. And in 1764 history repeated itself. The men appointed to replace him in Bengal had been just as greedy—and less effective. Once again the company's holdings in India were in trouble. Clive was offered a new and improved deal. If he would return to Bengal as both governor and commander in chief, his annual payment would be restored. He accepted. For the moment, Sulivan was driven out and Clive triumphant.

Many in the London elite could not stand Clive the outsider when he tried to buy his way into their ranks with money he made in India. The East India Company itself was bitterly divided over whether to embrace or reject him. Yet neither English nobility nor company stockholders (often enough the same people) could do without Clive the "heaven-born" leader when he was in India.

England could send ambitious men like Clive overseas and reap great benefit from their daring, but it did not know what to do with them once they succeeded and tried to take a leading role in English society. Charles Townshend, who would later play a key part in American history, is said to have sneered, "The fellow was right to transplant himself, he could not thrive on his native soil."

Similarly, England could ship thousands of settlers overseas to North America and anticipate rich rewards to the home country from the crops they would grow and the goods they would buy. But no English government could abide what it viewed as the selfish, immature behavior of the colonists. Instead of being a steady source of wealth and providing an outlet for the disgruntled, the colonies were proving to be a fertile ground for disturbing ideas.

Down in Virginia an eloquent, hot-tempered young lawyer named

Patrick Henry had already argued that a king who acted illegally, "far from being the father of his people, degenerates into a tyrant, and forfeits all rights to his subjects' obedience." These were the kinds of ideas that had led to civil war in England and chased Wilkes to France. Fortunately, they had been safely silenced since the great debates of 1647, when radicals had proposed the idea that all free Englishmen with a bit of property should be able to vote. In the American protests, and with mobs chanting Wilkes's name, that silence was ending.

Instead of providing an outlet for ambitious men and a steady source of wealth for the motherland, the colonies were increasing the burdens of England's rulers. Empire did not solve problems; it simply spread them around the entire globe.

CHAPTER 6

Slave or Free?

THE SPIRIT OF FREEDOM

George Grenville suffered from bad timing. Merchants in the colonies had done well during the Seven Years' War, since they had a large army to supply. As they prospered, they borrowed more and more in order to buy supplies. But when peace came, they had to cover their ballooning debts with shrinking earnings. The spectacular bankruptcy of one of the largest merchants in Boston in turn brought down other, smaller, tradesmen who counted on his business. Having to pay fees they had long avoided was just the wrong medicine for these ailing businessmen. As Benjamin Franklin calmly observed, Grenville's plan was simply bad economics: The more the colonists spent on taxes, the less money they would have to buy goods shipped from England. In the name of saving the English taxpayer, the prime minister would end up hobbling the English economy.

The debate on Grenville's plan quickly moved past these simple economic matters. James Otis noticed that it "set people a thinking, in six months, more than they had done in their whole lives before." They were thinking about slavery. After all, what right did Grenville, or Parliament, or the king himself, have to tax the colonies at all without their consent? As the Massachusetts General Assembly put it, "If taxes are laid upon us in any shape without ever having a legal representative where they are laid, are we not reduced . . . to the miserable state of tributary slaves?"

Why should the colonists have jumped to this conclusion? Why did any tax, even one that paid for their own protection, loom as the heavy arm of dictatorship? Why was slavery so present to their minds?

Americans were reading a seemingly endless stream of screaming, angry English political statements that made exactly that argument. The fact that Parliament was the kind of place in which a Clive and a Wilkes could buy seats, and from which they could be excluded by equally undemocratic manipulations, was not lost on critics in England. In fact, these skeptics formed a very alert, energetic, and suspicious group. In their endless pamphlets, letters, and books they kept returning to the same theme: Power corrupts; Parliament was corrupt and powerful; free men were in great peril. The flood of antigovernment literature moved quickly across the Atlantic. American readers saw the English government through the eyes of its most frightened, suspicious, and angry critics, and applied those insights to their own lives.

Many in Parliament argued there was no reason to give Americans a voice, since the people in cities such as Manchester had none, either. James Otis reversed that argument, saying if so many English were excluded from Parliament, "they ought" to be represented. But the fact that literate

Americans such as Otis knew the details of English history and law also meant that if Parliament made concessions to the Americans, it would be under more pressure to change its rules at home—which the majority of its representatives had no intention of doing.

The link between English writings and American beliefs was not limited

This cartoon pokes fun at England's financial problems, with Grenville failing miserably to balance "debts" and "savings" while a native, representing America, wears a sign saying "taxed without representation," and Britannia, symbol of England, sits sadly on the right. In satirical images such as this, people on both sides of the Atlantic took sides in the mounting conflicts. (LIBRARY OF CONGRESS)

to constitutional questions. Many American families, especially in New England, had fled from the England of Charles I, when Parliament seemed crushed and the foul king claimed he ruled as God's representative on Earth. Now, every ship landing in Boston brought new articles from the smartest, most articulate, most trusted people in England insisting that those evil days were returning once again. The Americans were poring over writings that read like fever dreams, political nightmares, and seeing in them the very beliefs that had sent their own ancestors across the ocean.

The fears of the colonists and their allies in England bordered on paranoia—they saw conspiracy everywhere. John Adams, for one, knew that his family had journeyed to America as a "Land of Promise," expecting the long-prophesied final battles between good and evil to begin soon. He still believed that their "Great Migration" was a crucial act in the "grand scene and design" through which God intended to save humanity. But if America was the homeland of the embattled fellowship of good, all the forces of evil, of slavery, must be gathering their strength to destroy it.

The religious drama of the end of time, the ultimate conflict of the saved and the damned, which had inspired Oliver Cromwell and John Winthrop in the 1600s, was still vivid in the minds of the heirs of the Puritans a century later. Adams and many others saw not merely bad laws being proposed but signs of truly satanic plots. In their minds the pattern of actions in London was more important, more revealing, than any specific act. For the design they perceived was the relentless effort of evil to conquer good, of dictatorship to enslave freedom.

Grenville's plan almost perfectly confirmed the suspicions of both English and American skeptics. He wanted to set up a permanent standing army in America, and he wanted to establish courts without local juries. His

The older John Adams in 1791, a portrait by the same Charles Willson Peale who painted Washington as a young Virginia colonel on page 30. Peale studied art in London, where his teacher was the transplanted American Benjamin West. (NATIONAL ARCHIVES AND RECORDS ADMINISTRATION)

plan could be read as providing direct support to the Church of England—so much like Charles I. And all this was to be paid for by taxes that the Americans had no chance to influence, modify, or approve. It was not hard for suspicious people to see what Grenville considered a simple, rational plan as the first step on the road to tyranny.

The judgment of those who considered this conflict as an evil conspiracy was often distorted. But they were not wrong to detect a kind of arrogant contempt in many English leaders. When Grenville's plan for a stamp tax was brought up for discussion in Parliament, few opposed it. Charles Townshend perfectly expressed the view of the Mother Country toward its troublesome, annoying colonies: "And now will those American children planted by our care, nourished up by our indulgence until they are grown to a degree of strength and opulence, and protected by our arms, will they grudge to contribute a mite to relieve us from the heavy weight of the burden we lie under?" Here in one sentence was the entire thinking behind Grenville's program: The Americans were selfish children who had the freedom to dispute having to pay their due only because of the protection offered by their parents. They had no rights; they simply had to wake up, grow up, and meet their responsibilities. Their very protests were a sign of their immaturity, their absolute dependence on England.

Hearing this, the heavyset Isaac Barré, the hero of Quebec, who had led Wolfe's men up the cliffs and paid with a battle wound, leaped to his feet and addressed the House of Commons. He could not stand this kind of small-minded, ignorant self-satisfaction, and he gave a short speech that, to this day, rings with his rough-hewn passion: "They planted with your care? No! Your oppressions planted 'em in America. They fled from your tyranny to a then uncultivated and un-hospitable country. . . . And yet, actuated by principles of true English liberty, they met all those hardships with pleasure. . . . They nourished by *your* indulgence? They grew by your neglect of 'em: as soon as you began to care about 'em, that care was exercised in persons to rule over 'em, who were perhaps the deputies to deputies to some member of this house—sent to spy out their liberty, to misrepresent their actions and to prey upon 'em. . . . They protected by *your* arms? They have nobly taken up arms in your defence."

In a ringing phrase, Barré contrasted the scheming, corrupt English sent to govern the colonies with the "sons of liberty" who lived there. Then, after rebutting Townshend's casual contempt point by point, he ended with prophetic words: "Believe me, remember I this day told you so, that same

Isaac Barré, as he was portrayed in a 1781 London magazine. If you look back at the Benjamin West painting of the dying Wolfe, page 50, Barré is in the center, holding his fallen leader in his lap.

(LIBRARY OF CONGRESS)

spirit of freedom which actuated that people at first, will accompany them still." He then abruptly stopped, perhaps to prevent himself from saying what he thought next—that someday the colonies would insist on their complete independence.

SLAVERY

Despite Barré's eloquence, the tax that would be collected every time an official piece of paper needed a governmental stamp—which Grenville had first mentioned in 1763—was approved by Parliament two years later.

Reaction against it in Massachusetts was predictable. But a French traveler happened to witness the most ferocious, and telling, response. He set out for Virginia's capital, Williamsburg, on May 30, 1765. Along the way he saw "three Negroes hanging from the gallows" for a small theft. He then stood next to a young Thomas Jefferson in the lobby of the House of Burgesses (the colony's governing body) and heard an astonishing speech. Patrick Henry rose to object to the new stamp tax and made a direct parallel between the present and the days of the English Civil War: "In former times Charles had his Cromwell, and he [Henry] did not doubt but that some good American would stand up, in favor of his country." In other words, a tax imposed on Americans was the kind of oppression that had led good Englishmen to bring down their king.

Whether it was John Adams in Boston or Patrick Henry in Williamsburg, Americans were intensely conscious of the civil war in which their ancestors had fought, and ever alert to the possibility that they would have to fight it again.

Only 39 of the usual 116 assembly members were present at the session, and with that reduced body Henry did more that just talk. He convinced them to pass a set of five firm resolutions objecting to the tax. On his deathbed an independence-minded Massachusetts lawyer named Oxenbridge Thacher, who had worked with James Otis in the writs of assistance case, heard about the Virginia Resolves. Weak as he was, he exclaimed, "They are men!"

Men, yes—slaveholding men. The anonymous traveler's report begins with the three hanged men, most probably slaves. That is a perfect counterpoint to Henry's eloquence speaking to a body of slaveholding men in the cause of liberty and freedom. Why would plantation owners, whose entire

This is a 1904 photograph of a portrait of Patrick Henry that was painted thirteen years earlier and hangs in the Capitol building in Washington. The artist tried to give a sense of Henry's passionate intensity. (LIBRARY OF CONGRESS)

livelihood depended on the involuntary, enforced labor of enslaved people, be so concerned about liberty and freedom, rights and corruption?

In Virginia, independence and slavery were strange twins. The money brought by tobacco plantations gave squires like George Washington and Thomas Jefferson freedom to think. Not having to scramble each day for money to meet another bill encouraged a sense of honor and independence. The tobacco barons also didn't have to worry, as did the lords in London, that the gin-soaked city mob might turn against them. There were no large cities and no mobs; there were only workers who had been stripped of all

Thomas Jefferson, as captured in a charcoal drawing. (NATIONAL ARCHIVES AND RECORDS ADMINISTRATION)

rights. But the presence of slaves was also a reminder: People could lose every protection, every right, and be reduced to a species of property. Slaves provided both a foundation for an appreciation of freedom and a dire warning of what could happen if that precious good was lost.

This knot, this tangle, was no simple case of hypocrisy. Though every human society, from the smallest groups living in the Amazon rain forest to the most sophisticated Greek, Roman, Chinese, or African kingdoms, practiced some form of slavery, the kind of slavery used in Virginia was relatively new.

In most older forms of slavery, slaves were not expected to be very productive. Often they were members of a household, who might be freed in old age. The presence of a slave showed off the status of a master; only rarely did the owner count on slaves to produce his wealth. But in the New World, slaves were imported in unheard-of numbers to provide manpower on the plantations that were crucial to the economies of the new colonies. Needed as work gangs, slaves were rarely freed, and their children were bred to continue this lifetime of enforced labor. Even this was a later development. Through much of the seventeenth century the tobacco crop was farmed by indentured servants—poor whites whose passage to the New World was paid in exchange for an agreement to be a servant for a finite period of years. Only in the 1700s did slaves purchased from Barbados and other Caribbean islands replace white indentures in the tobacco fields.

Ironically, having slaves made it easier for both wealthy planters and small farmers to think of freedom. The squires did not have to fear that they were importing poor people who, after a decade or so, would be turned loose, so they could feel more comfortable, more amiable, more democratic in spirit. Less-fortunate whites, knowing that there was a whole group of people—people of a different color and background—permanently beneath them in the social scale, could feel more similar to the grand planters. As foreign, and odious, as these beliefs and feelings seem to us now, we should not dismiss them. The appreciation of freedom that slavery bred in Virginia's planters was real and unmatched almost anywhere on Earth at the time; it was one of the most powerful forces driving the colonies toward independence and a more democratic government.

The squires' ability to cherish freedom even while they bought, sold, whipped, and had children with slaves was, in part, because they shared the mindset of the English. Washington, for example, argued that slaves should not be freed until they "had been educated to perceive what are the obligations of the state of freedom." Just as Townshend and Grenville viewed the colonists as children who must obey the rules wiser men made for them, Washington saw slaves as children who did not yet have the knowledge or training to handle freedom. And yet, in his will, Washington provided for the eventual liberation of his slaves—after his wife's death—and stipulated that young slaves who did not have living parents be taught to read and write.

Washington uneasily balanced the belief that slaves were not responsible enough for freedom with a certainty that they must be educated and freed. This queasy blend was matched in Jefferson by his sense of slavery's immorality and his terror at the thought of emancipation. In the seventeenth century, when the Virginia tobacco plantations were farmed by indentured servants, their masters had a very good way to discipline the workers: If an indentured person violated a rule, his or her term of service would be lengthened. The road to freedom came through obedience. But slaves already had a life sentence. Their masters' only enforcement tool was violence and death—the three men hanging outside the House of Burgesses. But that also created a great fear of the retribution the slaves were certain to exact, if they could.

In his *Autobiography* Jefferson famously wrote of slaves, "Nothing is more certainly written in the book of fate than that these people are to be free." These inspiring words are inscribed on his memorial in Washington. Yet his very next phrase—which is not on display—reads: "nor is it less certain that the two races, equally free, cannot live in the same government." And many years earlier he had determined that "deep-rooted prejudices entertained by the whites; ten thousand recollections, by the blacks, of the injuries they have sustained . . . will divide us into parties, and produce convulsions, which will probably never end but in the extermination of one or the other race." Slavery was abominable and yet it was a fact. Jefferson must have felt desire and possibly love for Sally Hemings, his enslaved mistress, yet he also experienced acute discomfort around slaves. He could not imagine slavery enduring, yet he could not picture a future in which free black and white people shared a nation. Jefferson was left with a fatalistic sense that slavery was an unshakable pillar of the economy, sustained by violence.

In the south the most ferocious advocates of liberty were slaveholders. In New England arguments about rights also served to protect smugglers. The American Revolution was born out of a moment when illegal and inhuman economies were linked with a passion for ideas of personal freedom and political liberty. This paradox stands at the very heart of all of American history.

Living in the New World gave Europeans opportunities they could not have enjoyed anywhere else. This chance to make money, to build new lives, exerted such a powerful pull that, to this day, it draws new immigrants from every corner of the globe. But ambition easily slides into greed, into bending rules of trade, into occupying Indian land, into buying and selling slaves. And yet that is only half of the story. A person who experiences greater opportunity also knows what it is to lose that possibility, to have that golden hope destroyed. The essence of the American conscience is the conviction that we must protect the right of others to pursue their own dreams.

Americans experience the driving hunger to succeed but also revere the idea that everyone else should also have that chance. Throughout our history we have alternated between phases in which we favor the dominant and the ambitious, and times in which we stand up for the rights of minorities and of the oppressed. That does not mean we should be cynics, sour about our own past. It would be simplistic to treat the founders' grand ideas about liberty and freedom as mere disguises for greed, masks for inhumanity. Rather, they were people of their time, who struck the balance between selfishness and idealism that made sense to them. It would take another century before Abraham Lincoln directly addressed the paradox the founders could not resolve. He set the future course of American history by declaring that a nation that both treated people as property and asserted that all men were equal could not endure.

CHAPTER 7

Networks

THE SPIRIT OF DEMOCRACY

The pathway to the American Revolution, one could argue, was simply a matter of networks and the speed at which information could be exchanged. In the eighteenth century it took three days to travel from Philadelphia to New York by stagecoach, and a week to get from New York to Boston on horseback. In 1776 there were only dirt roads linking the colonies from Boston to Savannah. A trip to England took a month to six weeks, so London was always dealing with slightly dated information about the colonies, and its responses and directives arrived months after any event. But each of the thirteen colonies communicated more with England, which set its key policies and dominated its trade, than with neighboring colonies that were hard to reach and, in any case, often economic rivals.

Only under extraordinary circumstances could these thirteen distinct colonies be brought together. In 1754, facing the threat of what would become the Seven Years' War, Benjamin Franklin, with the same Thomas Hutchinson who inspired the fury of James Otis, had developed a plan for uniting the colonies (not including Georgia). It was universally rejected. But if it was difficult for people to travel from one colony to another, or for the colonial governments to agree on anything, newspapers, letters—ideas

Benjamin Franklin created this famous image to urge Americans to join together at the time of the Seven Years' War. Very few people in America or England agreed with him. The colonies really were as divided as Franklin's snake. (LIBRARY OF CONGRESS)

in print—continued to move across the Atlantic, and up and down the Atlantic coast. It was easier for people throughout the colonies to exchange ideas than to meet each other in person.

When Grenville had first proposed his new tax on molasses, Massachusetts set up a committee of correspondence to share thoughts with other colonies. And as soon as newspapers in other colonies learned about the resolutions that Virginia had passed, they headlined the story. They didn't always get it right. In Rhode Island the *Newport Mercury* listed six resolves; the *Maryland Gazette* reported seven. The resolves they invented (or misreported) raised the temperature of the debate, for the made-up clauses asserted that anyone attempting to impose a tax without a colony's approval was "AN ENEMY TO THIS HIS MAJESTY'S COLONY." In other words, this was not just a debate over principles, it was a violation that colonists would defy and resist.

Inspired by what they thought Virginia had done, other colonies felt they had to be as bold in stating their objections to the stamp tax. Rhode Island went first, followed soon by seven others. The Massachusetts legislature urged representatives of all the colonies to meet in New York to discuss their common distress over the stamp tax.

When the Stamp Act Congress met in the fall

The Pennsylvania Journal and Weekly Advertiser *ran this image in October 1765. It showed what many Americans thought of Grenville's stamps: They were as deadly as a skull and crossbones.*
(LIBRARY OF CONGRESS)

of 1765, nine states sent representatives. At first they considered objecting merely on economic grounds—the approach Benjamin Franklin had first taken—but they did not stop there. As one concerned English observer noted, "A spirit of democracy is strong among them." By "democracy" he meant a belief in "the independency of the colonies."

The child Independence who had been born in James Otis's court case was growing. It was no longer just a gleam in the eyes of Bostonians. Now representatives of nine of the thirteen colonies were meeting together, and the rights of Englishmen were on all their minds. The congress resolved that it was "essential to the Freedom of a people, and the undoubted right of Englishmen, that no taxes be imposed on them, but with their own consent." Massachusetts went on to announce that there are "common rights of mankind" that anyone is "unalienably entitled to." Thomas Jefferson would later begin the Declaration of Independence with nearly identical words.

In opposition to the kind of arrogance and contempt Townshend had expressed in Parliament, the colonies were defining the beliefs that united them. But it was just as important that they were in contact at all. By writing to each other, covering each other's actions in the press, and meeting in person, vocal men and women throughout the colonies were also establishing links and connections with one another. These new information networks were the nervous system of a new nation.

MOBS

It was one thing for Grenville to come up with clever taxation schemes; it was another to enforce them in the colonies. He needed established, responsible men in each of the colonies to sell the new stamps and collect the fees.

To make the job more appealing, each of those officials was guaranteed a nice income in the bargain. Grenville asked knowledgeable colonists for nominations. Benjamin Franklin suggested an ally of his for Pennsylvania, the choice for Virginia was a friend of George Washington's, and for Massachusetts Thomas Hutchinson proposed his brother-in-law Andrew Oliver, who was already secretary of the colony. These choices looked fine in England. In the colonies, though, local opinion would speak louder than official calculation. When it came to an act like the stamp tax, the voice of the streets could be terrifyingly violent.

The stamp tax was due to take effect on November 1, 1765. During the summer a handful of brewers and shopkeepers, and the printer of the *Boston Gazette,* all of whom were opposed to the impending tax, met and gave themselves the name of the Loyal Nine—loyal, it would seem, to each other. As the group expanded, it took its new name from Barré's impassioned speech in Parliament—they became known as the Sons of Liberty.

Boston was a port town with a good share of rowdy men, young and old, black and white, who were eager for a fight. All of them looked forward to November 5, Guy Fawkes Day. This holiday celebrated the failure of a pro-Catholic plot to blow up Parliament, and thus was a great occasion to insult Catholics. Every year rival gangs from opposite sides of town held organized brawls over who would get to burn images of the devil and the pope. Up to four thousand men bashed each other with rocks, sticks, anything short of real arms. Most recently, a gang from the south end had come away the victor, and that was because of the fine leadership of a shoemaker named Ebenezer MacIntosh. The Nine approached MacIntosh. Could he use his ability to gather and control thousands of angry men to ensure that Oliver would not distribute the stamped papers? He agreed.

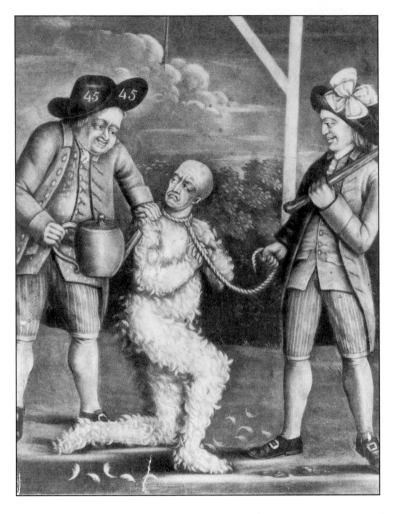

When the Americans tarred and feathered a British customs officer named John Malcolm in 1774, the assault was satirized in this print called "A New Method of Macarony Making." Though the event took place nine years after the Stamp Act riots, it shows how readily the Americans used violence and intimidation. The "45" in one American's hat refers to The North Briton 45, the controversial issue that caused Wilkes to flee to France. The large bow in the other hat is a symbol of the Sons of Liberty. Many saw the angry conflicts over "liberty" in London and America as part of the same international crisis.

A "macarony" was an elegantly dressed, fashionable young man, and, according to one theory, when General Braddock's uniformed troops saw a homely American soldier, a "Yankee Doodle Dandy," they made fun of him for just sticking "a feather in his cap" and calling it "macaroni"—fancy dress. Like the supporters of Wilkes who ignored the satire in Hogarth's caricature of their hero, the Americans turned the British ridicule into their own marching song. (LIBRARY OF CONGRESS)

Even as MacIntosh made his plans, the *Gazette* kept publishing accusations and insinuations about the tax, thus heating up the emotional temperature in Boston. Otis spread the rumor that Hutchinson and Bernard had suggested the idea of the tax to Grenville, and he boasted that he could point out the very room in which they had hatched the plot. By mid-August, Boston was boiling and MacIntosh was ready to act.

On the morning of August 14 a dummy of Andrew Oliver was strung up on a tree. Swaying in the breeze next to the body was a large boot with a devil climbing out of it. Everyone in Boston understood the message: Andrew Oliver was a tool of the evil Lord Bute. Lieutenant governor Hutchinson told the sheriff to remove the cloth body, but the crowd was too large and too ominous, and the sheriff would not risk his men to try. MacIntosh knew how to orchestrate his troops, for they carried the dummy right in front of the building where the colony's leaders were meeting, chanting as they went by. The mob marched on, down to a new building that Oliver was constructing. They destroyed it. Then they gathered in front of his home, on Oliver Street, cut off the dummy's head, and pelted the house with rocks. The mob moved on to Fort Hill and, using wood taken from the building they had demolished, burned the image of the man carefully selected to collect the stamp tax in Boston. Just to be sure that Oliver and Hutchinson got the message, the crowd then returned to ransack Oliver's home, swearing that they would kill him.

The riot that MacIntosh masterminded for the Loyal Nine was now the law in Boston. For when Governor Bernard asked the colonel of the militia to send a drummer to call out the troops, he was told that any such drum would be destroyed, and anyway, all potential drummers were probably part of the mob. The following day Oliver agreed not to accept the post of stamp distributor.

This etching from a 1784 book published in Germany shows the Bostonians' fury at the Stamp Act.
(LIBRARY OF CONGRESS)

Planted rumors, angry newspaper articles, violent mobs—these had more power in Boston than Grenville's plans. And then on Sunday, August 25, yet one more Boston voice was heard: The minister Jonathan Mayhew delivered a sermon. Mayhew drew the sharpest of contrasts between liberty—government with the consent of the governed—and slavery, rule by people "for their own interest, pleasure or profit, contrary to the will of the governed." Enslaved people, he urged his parishioners, do not need to remain passive and obedient. The minister did not say what they should do, but his incendiary message was delivered to a volatile city filled with men spoiling for a new fight. They heard him.

The next night MacIntosh's men were out in force. Stoked up on spiked punch and chanting about "liberty and property," one band looted the home and office of a colony official, while another rampaged through the elegant home of the comptroller of customs, smashing furniture, windows, and doors and cleaning out his wine cellar. The cobbler then gathered together his thugs and directed them toward the night's real entertainment: destroying the home of Thomas Hutchinson. In a full night of pillage they knocked down anything standing, slashed paintings, stole clothing, cash, and silverware, and were taking apart the slate roof when the sun rose and they had to disperse. Though everyone in Boston knew MacIntosh had stage-managed all the attacks, neither he nor anyone else was ever charged with a crime. In Boston the alliance of local forces could overrule any English law, unless London was willing to send over enough troops to enforce it.

Now the information links in the colonies worked in reverse. News of Virginia's resolves had inspired Massachusetts. Boston's ability to intimidate Oliver into resigning now encouraged Rhode Islanders to organize their own Sons of Liberty to burn dummies, demolish houses, and cow any potential stamp distributors into quitting. It worked. Colony by colony the men who had looked forward to the lucrative post resigned rather than lose their homes and property. By November 1 only in Georgia, where the governor had troops at his command, was there any chance that Grenville's new law could be enforced.

Since resistance to the stamp tax was part of the drive toward the American Revolution, it is easy for a modern reader to side against Grenville's laws. But MacIntosh's rioters, the ineffectual militia, the silent judges, the goading press, and inflammatory sermons have a lot in common with some of the worst aspects of later American history, such as vigilantes and lynch mobs. Boston showed all the ways local forces could intimidate and silence those whose opinions influential people do not like. Just as in Virginia slavery was the foundation of the passion for freedom, in Boston the cause of liberty was advanced by carefully planned terror.

The flow of information from colony to colony, Sons of Liberty to Sons of Liberty, was not limited to political resolves or prescriptions for violence. Starting in 1765, Massachusetts had encouraged people to fight against Grenville's act by simply not buying the imported items that would carry new taxes. Widows could choose plainer clothes; drinkers could stick with American beer; ladies could forgo "gaudy, butterfly, vain, fantastic, and expensive dresses brought from Europe" and instead wear "decent plain dresses made in their own country." A good part of the burden for making these choices fell on women, who would have to give up items they wanted, and sew and make the alternatives themselves. Many did. As the nonimportation movement grew, so did the range of people becoming invested in the conflict with England. From the sailor who joined in a managed riot to the woman who designed her own dress, the challenge that began in lawyers' debates was becoming a larger cause.

Franklin Addresses Parliament

How would London react to the defiance in the colonies? This question became more complicated over the summer of 1765, because Grenville lost power. As he left office, Grenville urged the king not to change his approach to the colonies, "the richest jewel of his crown." George III replaced him with the ailing Duke of Cumberland, his uncle. But on October 31, the night before the Stamp Act was to take effect, Cumberland died.

The new government was run by Charles Watson-Wentworth, Lord Rockingham, a wealthy landlord. Rockingham was interested only in what leading businessmen thought should be done about the colonies. Just as Franklin had first suggested, the whole matter of Grenville's program could be seen as an economic miscalculation. Franklin himself crossed the Atlantic to make that point.

When he addressed Parliament, Franklin was sixty years old and the most famous American in the world. Like Washington, Franklin had spent his life studying how to get ahead, how to improve himself. "God," he famously wrote, "helps them that help themselves." But while Washington copied down rules originally printed for French aristocrats, Franklin crafted a set of maxims that, to this day, sound completely American. In fact, they went a long way toward defining what it is to be American. In *Poor Richard's Almanac* he reduced life to a set of startlingly clear equations. "Haste makes waste." "No gains without pains." "Search others for their virtues, thy self for thy vices." "Diligence is the mother of good luck." Hard work and thrift produce money, honor, success. Laziness and time wasting result in poverty, sickness, misery.

Franklin stripped the challenges of life down to the simplest and most practical choices. No need to worry about God's plans. No reason to kow-

In this 1761 image Benjamin Franklin is surrounded by references to his scientific interests and inventions—a bolt of lightning, instruments, even a book titled Electric Expts. *Franklin's experiments impressed Europeans and made him the representative American—the person who stood for the best of his homeland.*

tow to the powerful. Your life is in your hands, right here, right now. These pragmatic rules were a perfect distillation of what many white Americans and some free blacks were experiencing in their own lives. Though Franklin's sayings were not at all political, they were in a sense revolutionary. For they crystallized what was different for free people living in America. Life was what you made it, not what you were born into.

Following his own advice, Franklin had made his fortune by the time he was forty-two, and retired from business. Philadelphia was America's largest city, and Pennsylvania its second-largest colony (300,000 slaves made Virginia the most populous). Intensely involved in the politics of this crucial colony, Franklin was just now returning to London for his second stint as an advocate for the interests of Pennsylvania.

Franklin's speech was taken down by a stenographer and quickly published. His view was supported by a detailed analysis, undertaken by one of Rockingham's wealthy merchant advisers, of the disastrous economic effects of the Stamp Act. In March Parliament revoked the act.

Parliament responded to the kind of pragmatism Franklin advocated, but without granting that the colonists had been right to protest. Instead, it passed a Declaratory Act that confirmed its absolute authority over the colonies. The great orator and leader William Pitt, who had organized England's victorious campaigns in the Seven Years' War (and for whom Pittsburgh is named), thundered, "The force of this country can crush America to atoms."

Americans were glad to be rid of the stamp tax, but they understood what Parliament was really saying: "We may have been wrong this time, but we are in charge, and if you know what is good for you, you will play nice and be quiet." The influential Virginia planter George Mason perfectly cap-

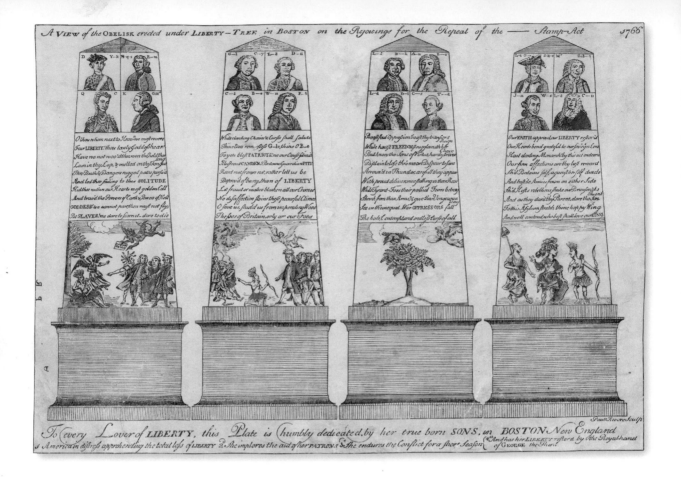

Paul Revere created these amazing obelisks to stand on Boston Common as a celebration of the repeal of the Stamp Act. The pillars were lit from the inside so that they would glow. Each of the four sides showed stages of the successful fight and highlighted English friends of America. Among the heads are Isaac Barré, William Pitt, and John Wilkes, and also, strangely, Charles Townshend and George III.

(LIBRARY OF CONGRESS)

tured Parliament's tone. He heard them lecturing "in the authoritative style of a master to a school-boy. 'We have, with infinite difficulty and fatigue got you excused this one time; pray be a good boy in the future; do what Papa and Mama bid you.'" If you obey, we "'will love you, and praise you, and give you pretty things.'"

The colonies had the power of local violence and general boycotts. Parliament insisted that it had the final right to set policies for the colonies. The question no one yet wanted to decide was which of these was making a hollow boast—the headstrong colonists spoiling for a fight they were sure to lose, or the self-important members of Parliament asserting authority they had shown no ability to enforce.

CHAPTER 8

Edges of Empire

"THE INDIANS' HUNTING GROUND"

*I*t is the summer of 1769, and Daniel Boone has been traveling with five other companions since May. He first met one of them, John Findley, fourteen years earlier while serving with General Braddock, and ever since then he has heard tales of the fabled land of Kenta-ke, west of the Appalachians. Findley told of lands so rich and fertile that any man and his family could prosper, of game just waiting to be bagged, of ducks and geese killed by rapid currents lying by riverbeds as if on display. However much he exaggerated, Findley truly has visited the lands he described. Boone's nephew later claimed that the famous Kentucky bluegrass—which is not native to North America—was spread from the English hay that Findley used to cushion his trade goods when he first explored the area. Boone tried to find his way to this wonderful land two years earlier but failed. Now he is back and about to change American history.

Findley has led his party to the great V-shaped notch in the Appalachians that Thomas Walker named the Cumberland Gap after the very same Duke of Cumberland who died just before the Stamp Act was to take effect. For thousands of years the Cumberland Gap has offered a passage to animals, then Indians, and now to Boone and his party—a pathway past the mountain chain and out to the west. In the next seventy-five years an estimated 300,000 settlers will follow in their path. Yet for Boone this is not yet the place he has come to find.

It is only when Boone passes through the gap and climbs the 700-foot hill known as Pilot Knob that he finally sees that Findley has been telling the truth. Stretched out below him like a flat, lush, and welcoming carpet are the lands Findley described. Awed, humbled by what he has found, Boone exclaims, "We are as rich as Boaz of old, having the cattle of a thousand hills." He is speaking in the language of the Old Testament, likening himself to the wealthy great-grandfather of King David. The territory opening before him truly is a promised land.

Boone's first expedition to Kentucky is a hunting trip, and for six months he has success beyond imagination. There are as many buffalo and elk for food and clothing as any hunter could want, and each deer they shoot, skin, and pack promises a nice sale when they return home. By December 22 they have hundreds of pounds' worth of skins. But as Boone and one other hunter return to camp, they are ambushed by a Shawnee war party. Boone does everything he can to alert the other four at camp to scatter with their skins, but to no avail. The Shawnee, not the colonists, will profit from the long hunt.

Captain Will, as the Shawnee leader is known, sends Boone home with a bit of equipment and a warning: "Don't come here any more, for this is the Indians' hunting ground, and all the animals, skins and furs, are ours. And if you are so foolish as to venture here again, you may be sure the wasps and yellow-jackets will sting you severely."

* * *

To Boone the bluegrass land beyond the Cumberland Gap was a kind of biblical place of milk and honey, an El Dorado for hunters and farmers. To the Shawnee it was private hunting ground, to be protected first with warnings and then with weapons. This kind of encounter is exactly what Grenville's Proclamation Line was designed to prevent. The failure of this last part of his program was as central to America's future as the protests over the stamp tax.

Strictly enforcing the original barrier against new settlement would have required far more than the 10,000 troops Grenville requested. In 1763, the first year of the ban on crossing the mountains, a mob in Paxton, Pennsylvania, made that clear. Furious over the Indian attacks in Pontiac's Rebellion, they found and killed six friendly Christian Indians; then, as Benjamin Franklin described it, they found fourteen more and "men, women, and little children—were every one inhumanly murdered! In cold Blood!" Their numbers swelled from 50 to 250 as the Paxton Boys headed off for Philadelphia, where another 140 converted Indians had taken shelter. The mob was not intimidated in the slightest when they neared the homes of wealthy Quakers who wanted to protect the Indians. Instead, they threatened to kill them, too.

Franklin went with a delegation of six men to deter the crowd from entering the city. In the end they did disperse. But just as in Boston, where a mob could set its own rules of trade, in the backcountry armed settlers with few scruples about killing Indians, and even fewer concerns about lines written on maps thousands of miles away, made their own laws.

Even without bloody events such as the Paxton murders, Grenville's Proclamation Line was doomed. By 1766 over 500 families were living west of the line, near Fort Pitt. When the English tried to drive them away, "double the number" came back. In turn, some of the wealthiest and most powerful men in England had invested in companies claiming title to the very lands Grenville reserved for the Indians. Even if they could not at once overturn his law, they would fight hard to make sure it could not be enforced.

Leading Americans such as George Washington were even more resistant to the line. He had, after all, helped to start the Seven Years' War while employed by the Ohio Company, which was speculating in western lands. As he wrote to a surveyor who was working for him, "I can never look upon that Proclamation in any other light (but this I say between ourselves) than as a temporary expedient to quiet the minds of the Indians & [one that] must fall of course in a few years."

By the time Boone headed for the Cumberland Gap, the Proclamation Line was in tatters. Like the tangled issues of slavery and freedom, the matter of the western lands was a crossing place of greed, violence, racial prejudice, and an unquenchable hunger on the part of people like Boone to live independent lives. Boone himself realized that he had pursued Indians "as I would now follow the tracks of a ravenous animal." He did not mean to imply that the Indians were subhuman but, rather, to show the depth of his own bloodlust. He did not defend his actions as righteous, for he understood that he had been "waging a war of intrusion" on the native nations. Had he lost that war or been killed, he would have accepted that as just. For the Indians had every right to defend their lands. Like Jefferson's view of slavery, this is simultaneously an expression of regret and of historical necessity. It was horrible, Boone seemed to say, but it could not have been any other way. That is both true and tragic. For only the English could

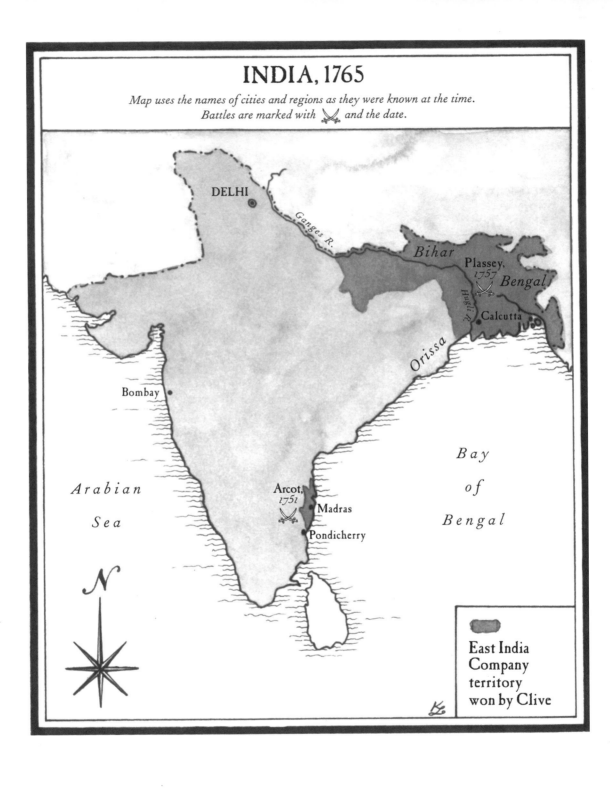

INDIA, 1765

Map uses the names of cities and regions as they were known at the time.
Battles are marked with ⚔ and the date.

DELHI

Ganges R.

Bihar

Plassey,
1757

Bengal

Hugli R.

Calcutta

Orissa

Bombay

Arabian

Sea

Bay

of

Bengal

Arcot,
1751

Madras

Pondicherry

N

🟫

East India
Company
territory
won by Clive

have held back the intruders and protected the hunting grounds, and they were both too far away and too eager for their own profits to make any significant difference.

RULERS OF BENGAL

The *Kent,* carrying Robert Clive back to India, reached Madras on April 10, 1765. As the ship rocked in the restless waters, he wrote an urgent letter to the new chairman of the East India Company in London. With Clive once again on the rise, Sulivan had been replaced. Based on what he now knew of local conditions, Clive believed that the "whole Mogul empire is in our hands. . . . We must indeed become Nabobs ourselves." "We" meant the company. Clive was proposing that a trading partnership rule an empire. He made the extraordinary suggestion because he knew that English and East India Company soldiers together were the most powerful army in all of India, and that even the Mogul emperor needed their support.

In July Clive set off from Calcutta to meet the emperor, taking with him an entourage designed to awe all who saw him. In addition to two barbers and a full complement of personal servants, he brought an elephant, hawks, horses, and English hunting dogs. To make sure that the Indians understood that he had the status and power of a ruler, he purchased a tiger and added it to the menagerie. Clive was not merely showing off, he was staging a kind of play. For when he met up with Shah Alam II, he orchestrated a ceremony in which the emperor stood above him—Clive and the company were serving the heir of the great Moguls. That was to reassure everyone that he knew the rules, knew how things were done in India. In exchange for a military

Benjamin West's painting of the ceremony in which Clive received the grant of rights from Shah Alam was another fanciful reconstruction. For Wolfe's death West showed tragic heroism; for Clive's triumph he painted a scene of formality and exotic splendor. For a time it hung in one of Clive's homes near London. West himself went on to succeed Reynolds as the head of the Royal Academy.

alliance, the emperor made the company into the tax collector and in effect ruler of the provinces of Bengal, Bihar, and Orissa. Robert Clive, the rascal son of a struggling lawyer, had conquered a wealthy region and delivered it to his firm to run. He confidently predicted that the tax revenues would bring in 2 million pounds, or 320 million modern dollars, of additional profit every year.

   With Bengal in his hands, Clive set out to take control of the English in India. One after another officials, merchants, and soldiers—most notably John Johnstone—had followed his earlier example and made off with

John Johnstone, seated with his cousins Betty Johnstone and Miss Wedderburn, as painted around 1790 by Sir Henry Raeburn.   (GIFT OF MRS. ROBERT W. SCHUETTE.
IMAGE COPYRIGHT BOARD OF TRUSTEES NATIONAL GALLERY OF ART, WASHINGTON)

extravagant payoffs. Even those who did not negotiate direct "gifts" from Indian nobles browbeat them into ruinous trade concessions. Now that he was in a position of leadership, Clive sincerely tried to put a stop to the very practices he had made infamous. The result was a clash as dangerous as any he had faced in battle.

It is exactly as if Washington had taken vast stretches of Ohio land for himself but then insisted that every new settler be scrupulous in his dealings with the Indians and content himself with a small farm. The English in India reacted with the same outrage as settlers certainly would have in America. When a group of army officers threatened to quit, Clive faced them down. That seemed to take the last of his strength.

Ever since he had first arrived in India, fighting battles had saved Clive from his intense depressions. But there was another side to that seesaw: After each triumph he experienced a new bout of physical pain and emotional exhaustion. Early on, he began to use opium to try to quell the pain and govern his emotions, which only made the next attack worse. By January 1767, after delivering Bengal to his company and doing his best to control the greed of company officers, Clive collapsed. Endlessly sobbing, unable to think, read, or write, he consoled himself with ever larger doses of the drug. One last time Clive sailed off for England to recover, to be hailed for his triumphs, and to face the powerful friends and influential allies of the men he had tried to discipline.

In America, England had disobedient colonists spreading across the Alleghenies and restlessly asserting that they were not children. Precisely because the colonists knew their English history, they demanded the full rights of Englishmen. The question was when they would go too far, and

These golden vanki, *armbands, were brought back from India by John Johnstone. They give a hint of the treasure he accumulated there.* (CT47644, V&A IMAGES/VICTORIA AND ALBERT MUSEUM)

London would have to send an army to subdue them. In India an English company was now governing a wealthy region. The company officials were behaving more and more like local princes and, some feared, might even corrupt England itself. The question was whether a trading company was capable of ruling an area in which the entire population obeyed laws, observed customs, spoke languages, and prayed to gods alien to the English. The more the English empire expanded, the less sure anyone was about how it should be run.

CRISIS

CHAPTER 9

Half Measures

"WHAT IS ENGLAND NOW?"

The news of Clive's brilliant acquisition in India inspired investors in England. If Lord Plassey, a great leader who was wealthy beyond imagining, was certain that running Bengal would add millions to the company's earnings, who could doubt him? Within a year of his return, the price of what had once been 100 pounds', 16,000 modern dollars', worth of stock soared from 164 pounds, 26,240 dollars, to 273 pounds, 43,680 dollars. This was not just excitement—it was a kind of frenzy. Everyone from wealthy English lords and government ministers to reckless Scottish stock-market speculators, from eager Jewish traders at the Amsterdam stock exchange to newly rich East India Company directors, rushed to buy up the stock. As the price soared, the stakes grew higher, and higher, and higher. Still locked in their grim battle for control of the company, supporters of Clive and backers of Sulivan competed to purchase ever more of the inflated stock, raising the price still further.

Though it sounds unbelievable today, when there are stock markets in every country trading shares in thousands of companies, in 1770 the entire interconnected world market in which investors speculated came to rest on the value of East India Company shares. Traders began experimenting with the kinds of bets that are still used to this day: guessing what the price of shares would be at a specific time in the future (called "futures"), betting that the price would go up (a "long" position) or down (selling "short"). More and more investors were putting up only a small part of the money needed to purchase stocks and borrowing the rest. They were so sure that East India Company stock would continue to rise that they expected to be able to repay their loans and make a profit by reselling the stock when it was worth more. Bets built on bets built on bets, making many investors rich and able to buy more stock, and lend more money to others. This bubble of giddy speculation soon affected the colonists in America.

Proud Virginia squires, for example, paid for their mansions and lavish lifestyles by drawing on credit from the Scottish merchants who bought and sold their tobacco. The Scots, in turn, were now using every pound they had, and much more that they borrowed, to bet on East India Company shares. As long as tax income from Bengal flowed into company coffers, the Scots would be rich and able to lend ever more money to the Virginians, to pay for more carriages, wine cellars, and slaves. But that also meant that the Virginians' sense of independence was a complete sham—their security was entirely dependent on people they had never met, in places they could hardly imagine, on the other side of the globe.

The Virginians did not realize how vulnerable they were—people caught up in a boom seldom do—but some in England were raising doubts about the astonishing loot flooding into the country from India. Was this wealth truly legal? What was it doing to the nation?

"What is England now?" one writer questioned. "A sink of Indian wealth . . . a country run by horse-races! A gaming, robbing, wrangling, railing nation without principles, genius, character, or allies." In a new government shuffle, Rockingham lost out and Pitt—now the Earl of Chatham—returned. He, too, was disturbed by what he was hearing and seeing. "The riches of Asia have been poured in upon us," he lamented. "Without connections, without any natural interest in the soil, the importers of foreign gold have forced their way into Parliament by such a torrent of private corruption as no hereditary fortune could resist." In fact, returning India hands were entering the House of Commons in ever greater numbers: five in 1767, twenty-six in 1774, forty-five out of the total of 558 members ten years later. One after another—for example, the Johnstone brothers: George, John, and William (who took his wealthy wife's name, Pulteney)—purchased seats. And soon there was a faction in Parliament using John's Indian money to protect their interests in government, just as they banded together to fight for control of the East India Company.

The head of England's own government was expressing the kinds of fears that haunted both angry critics in England and fearful colonists in America. If Parliament could be bought, how could anyone trust the laws it passed? No wonder the colonies wanted to be sure they consented to their own taxes. How could they entrust their rights to a rotten body in which bribes spoke louder than principles?

But Pitt wanted Parliament to be run by people with "connections," with a "natural interest in the soil," with "hereditary fortunes"—in other words, not by people across the ocean, not by self-made newcomers, not by outsiders. And it was Scots like the Johnstones, Irishmen like Sulivan, declining families like the Clives, even Jewish traders and merchants, who were rising along with the East India Company. The company provided a new horizon,

This cartoon makes fun of the ragged, deformed Scots, called Caledonians, who were taking advantage of Lord Bute's rise to power make their fortunes. The image of a boot hanging from the tavern at the left is the clue—everyone understood the pun of "boot" for "Bute." In fact, Lord Bute did favor his countrymen, such as the Johnstones, and gave them many plum positions in North America. But even after he lost power, Scots eagerly set out for India, the Caribbean, and North America.

(P282804, COURTESY THE BRITISH MUSEUM)

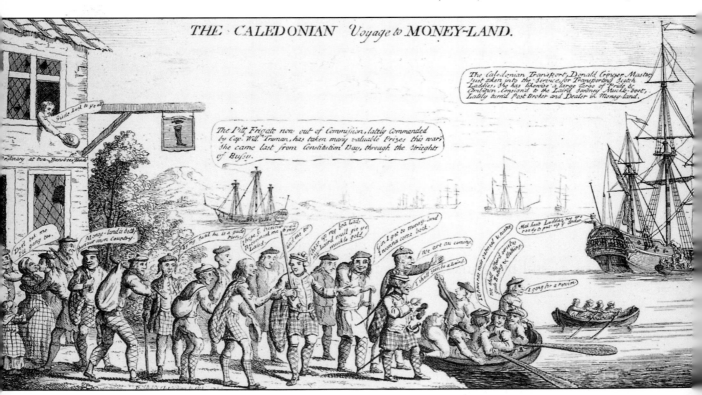

This formal portrait shows Lady Clive in later life. Despite her appealing personality and great wealth, she was never fully accepted into English society.

(THE POWIS COLLECTION, POWIS CASTLE (THE NATIONAL TRUST NTPL)

Lord Clive, as painted in 1773. This is the image of Clive at his most confident and established. Nathaniel Dance painted both of these portraits.

(NPG 39, COURTESY THE NATIONAL PORTRAIT GALLERY, LONDON)

a new frontier for ambition very much like the New World across the Atlantic. Yet the highest levels of English society remained closed to all these successful newcomers. Clive, for example, bought home after gorgeous home in the most fashionable districts in and around London, and his wife was an appealing, charming woman, but the cream of society never called on her. Money flooding into England from India was as alien as protests about rights from America. Pressures from the edges of empire were unsettling England itself.

Pitt also had a more practical concern. With all this money flowing from India to the East India Company, he thought some of it should be coming to the government. He hit upon a familiar idea: Since the English army had helped win glorious battles for the company, the company should help to cover its costs. This was exactly the plan Grenville had proposed for North America—let those protected by the English army pay for it. Unlike the colonists, though, the company was willing to work out a deal. For an annual tax payment of 400,000 pounds, or 64 million modern dollars, Pitt agreed not to press the question of exactly what a trading company was doing acting as a government. If profits continued at anything like the pace Clive predicted, this was a small price to pay.

This compromise payment was suggested by a new minister with fiscal responsibilities, Charles Townshend. Townshend was eager to resolve any problems with the East India Company, as he, like many other high officials, owned the booming stock and he certainly did not want to see its value decline. He also had another army to worry about: the 10,000 troops Grenville had stationed in North America. The latest estimate was that in the forthcoming year they would cost the government exactly the same amount as the company had just agreed to pay, 400,000 pounds.

Townshend convinced Parliament to adopt a scheme that addressed all his concerns but solved none of them. This had as much to do with his personality as with his judgment.

Townshend was gifted with a sharp tongue and a quick wit, and he had not the least bit of judgment in using them. As a nineteen-year-old college student, he had spent an evening making outrageous statements about one of his classmates while literally poking his tongue into his cheek to make sure everyone knew he was joking. But the rather thick James Johnstone, yet another of the brooding Scottish brothers, did not catch on. When someone explained to him that he had been the butt of a series of insults, the furious Johnstone challenged Townshend to a fight. At this Townshend panicked, turned pale, and only barely managed to soothe the angry boy. Both his ability to whip off round after round of amusing insults and his terrible judgment in directing them at the one person most likely to take serious offense were typical of Townshend.

There were a number of reasons for Townshend's unerring ability to be clever when it did no good, and insulting when it caused great harm. For one, he probably suffered from epilepsy, and while he had phases in which he was the wittiest, most brilliant speaker in all of Parliament, his constant struggle to control himself might easily have diminished his ability to sense how he was affecting others. But more to the point, he had a very troubled relationship with his wealthy, difficult father, who tightly controlled the family purse strings. Over and over Townshend ignored and defied his father until he really needed money. In desperate straits, he would then beg, humble himself, and write endless fawning letters until his father covered his debts. This pattern kept repeating until he married well, obtained his own fortune, and could ignore his father. Townshend alternated between defying authority and abjectly insisting on his perfect loyalty.

Townshend viewed the American colonists as rebellious children. Playing the part of his own father, he decided that they must be governed with a stern hand and a very tight financial fist. Just like his barrage of freshman insults, this approach was almost perfectly suited to infuriate the people who were likely to make Townshend's life miserable and England's rule impossible.

Townshend proposed a new variant of Grenville's plan. Again taxes would be added to the prices of certain specific items imported into the colonies—this time, lead, glass, paper, colored paint, and tea. And a new, more able group of commissioners would be established in Boston to make sure all customs fees were collected. He thought that these new charges would not cause too much of a problem because most colonists would not need the items, so they would not have to pay anything new. That was true. But it also meant England could not expect to make much from the fees. Townshend himself expected the government to earn only about 40,000 pounds, 6.4 million modern dollars, one tenth of the amount needed by the army.

Townshend's plan for North America was likely to annoy Americans without yielding the income England needed. His compromise with the company brought needed cash without dealing with the real problem of how to manage the newly acquired responsibilities in India. Both were half measures, and it was anyone's bet which would fail first.

A FARMER WRITES, AND THE "MAN OF THE REVOLUTION" SPEAKS

Surprisingly, the Americans did not at first react strongly to Townshend's new decrees. If anything, merchants spoke up to discourage people from boycotting the goods with new taxes. In a series of essays called "Letters from a Farmer in Pennsylvania," a man who was actually a wealthy, educated lawyer counseled patience. John Dickinson suggested that Americans "behave like dutiful children who have received unmerited blows from a beloved parent." This was seemingly the very opposite of the language of independence. But it was not.

Dickinson wrote in a calm, deliberate fashion. Cautioning against any "hot, rash, disorderly proceedings," he set a tone that was a complete rejection of the riots organized by MacIntosh and the Boston mob. That is one reason for the popularity of his writings among established Americans. For his letters were quickly reproduced in twenty-one out of the twenty-five newspapers then publishing. The colonial press was proving to be an effective way of spreading ideas. And after he reassured and calmed his readers, Dickinson made it clear that the fees in the Townshend plan were taxes, exactly like Grenville's Stamp Act. He grasped what Townshend actually had intended: The point of the charges was to assert Parliament's authority, not simply to earn money. Dickinson was telling his fellow Americans to agree to show a childlike humility, so long as they thought with adult clarity. As people across the thirteen colonies read his sober, insightful prose, they gained a deeper sense of being in a common situation, of having a common cause, of not being children at all.

If any place in America was likely to take the "hot, rash" path, it was Boston. But at first the city was quiet. A series of motions to support a local boycott was defeated. Doing just the opposite of what might have been expected, in January 1768 the Massachusetts legislature refused to send a new letter to the other colonies to make a common protest against the new fees. Governor Bernard was still wary, and he was right to be, for the most gifted politician in North America was using his skills to ignite his slumbering city, and it would be a foolish man who bet against Samuel Adams.

Like his cousin John, Sam came from a family that was not well off but valued education. But while John had turned his training at Harvard into a promising career in law, Sam was better known at the same school for drinking than for studying. In fact, he never did well in any of the series of jobs he held, and he was often in debt. Yet he had one great passion, and one great gift: He was devoted to political causes, and he was a brilliant organizer. Adams belonged to every small group, club, or party whose ideas he supported, and he became a master of the very same techniques that had worked so well in the Stamp Act protests. Though no one then or since has been able to prove it, he may well have been the one to coordinate the links between the established Sons of Liberty and MacIntosh's rough men.

Adams fed the press the kinds of angry arguments that stirred readers. At the same time, he enjoyed bantering with workingmen. He was said to be friends with every good workman in town. He would sit for hours in smoke-filled rooms, drinking and mapping strategies with other politicians. Though he hardly knew how to ride a horse, when he realized he needed support from farmers, he figured out how to win their trust. Adams worked, and worked, and worked to establish the connections he needed, so that when it came time to act, his side was unstoppable. It was that dogged effort and organizational skill that made Jefferson call him "truly the Man of the Revolution." Now Adams's cause was to get the Massachusetts legislature to change its mind, and to send out a letter to the other colonies in support of common action.

Patrick Henry had been able to pass his resolves because most of the Virginia legislators had already gone home. Sam Adams used the same trick. He waited until the end of the session, when the more conservative farmers had left, and reintroduced his bill. This time it passed. When the Massachusetts letter went out, Virginia joined in. And the English did their part—just as Adams hoped, they overreacted.

The strains of managing an empire were showing in London, where one lord after another was being shuffled in and out of important posts. William

Pitt collapsed, and Townshend himself died before his acts took effect. By the time London read the letter Adams had gotten his assembly to send, Wills Hill, Lord Hillsborough, was responsible for the colonies. Sam Adams could not have invented a more perfect opponent.

Benjamin Franklin had a particular gift for getting along with people. Yet he and Hillsborough detested each other—which is a strong indication of why Hillsborough was precisely the wrong man to deal with the colonies. Franklin felt that the lord treated him with a kind of sneering "anger and contempt." In turn, the usually genial American saw Hillsborough as "deceitful," conceited (for no reason), obstinate, and wrong-headed. Hillsborough had a personal passion for limiting the growth of the colonies. In great part this was because he owned huge tracts of land in Ireland. He much preferred English settlers to go there, as his tenants, rather than to North America, as troublemakers.

With Hillsborough managing affairs in London and Adams doing the same in Boston, events moved quickly. Both were ready, eager, for a fight, and each gave the other just the right provocation. The lord insisted that the Massachusetts assembly take back what it had said in the letter or be dissolved, and also that the governors of the other colonies do the same. This not only encouraged colonies to endorse Adams's letter, it revived the flagging boycott movement in New England.

Once again Americans were urged to forgo English products and to make their own. One newspaper after another reported on the long ride of a man named Henry Lloyd. That was because "his clothes, linen, shoes, stockings, boots, gloves, hat, wig . . . were all manufactured . . . in New England." As Dickinson had predicted, "We never can be made an independent people except by Great Britain herself; and the only way for her to do it is to make us frugal, ingenious, united, and discontented." Hillsborough accomplished exactly that, and then Adams did the rest.

Of all the ill-considered half measures in Townshend's plan, the one most likely to cause an explosion was putting the headquarters of the new customs officials in Boston. This was an invitation to disaster. Officials with the assignment to be rigorous in pursuit of smugglers were planted in a town that had shown it would use every means just short of murder to silence anyone who interfered with its own ways of doing business. On June 10, 1768, the inevitable conflict began.

CHAPTER 10

Liberty

THE *LIBERTY*

John Hancock was a merchant, a member of the Sons of Liberty, and a notorious smuggler. In May a ship of his named the *Liberty* arrived in port with a cargo of good wine. As two customs officials checked, twenty-five barrels were unloaded and Hancock paid the required fees. With the hold empty, the *Liberty* was loaded with whale oil and tar, all normal business in the port. But a month later one of the officials, Thomas Kirk, reported that the inspection day had been anything but peaceful. After refusing a bribe, he had been shoved into a room on the ship, and while he heard many more than twenty-five barrels being taken off, he was warned to keep silent. No one was quite sure if Kirk was telling the truth, but the new commissioners saw a chance to make an example of Hancock.

On June 10, 1768, the *Liberty* was seized, and under guard from a warship, it was dragged away from the port and out into Boston Harbor. The locals standing on the pier first tried to prevent the seamen from taking away the ship, then, that night, spread the word. Thousands of men filled the streets of Boston looking for customs officials to terrorize. That was just the start. Within a week Bernard felt that the Sons of Liberty were in control of Boston. And when the Massachusetts legislature refused to rescind the letter protesting the Townshend Acts, the governor gave his opponents new fuel for their fires—for he disbanded the assembly. He had but one option left to establish some kind of control: ask London to send troops to Boston. By

Paul Revere etched this woodcut showing eight British warships in Boston Harbor overseeing the landing of British soldiers in the city.   (LIBRARY OF CONGRESS)

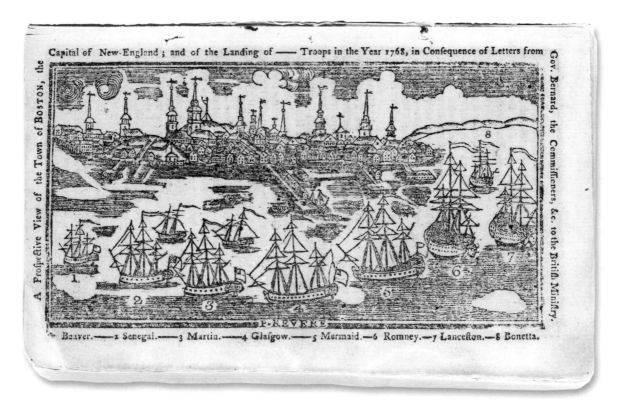

August word of his decision had leaked to the press. And on October 1 a line of warships entered the harbor. Boatload by boatload, two armed regiments of soldiers in full uniform with muskets and bayonets entered the city. To the harsh beat of their drums, they marched ahead and began to take their positions.

Sam Adams and his allies in the press now had visual proof of the nature of their enemy. Seeing soldiers on the streets of a city is terrifying. It is an intrusion of might, of force, in a place that just the day before was home. No matter how well behaved the troops, no matter how warranted their presence, people feel a sense of violation, of fear, and of anger. It is an "invasion," one paper screamed, an "occupation." The most extreme fears of those who felt their liberty was in danger were taking shape before their eyes. The legislature prevented from meeting, a tax imposed from London, soldiers in the street—the final days of evil seemed to have arrived. And then it got worse.

Ever since he had dared to speak out in *The North Briton*, John Wilkes had been as much of a hero to Americans such as Sam Adams as he was to London's poor. Now, as Boston felt the weight of London's power, the city's attention was riveted on Wilkes. At first the news was encouraging. In 1768 Wilkes returned to England from France, and in March he was elected to Parliament. Americans who were in the midst of their own conflict with the English government were thrilled at the return of the hero of the cause of liberty. The town of Wilkes-Barre, Pennsylvania, was given half of its name in his honor (the other half is taken from Colonel Isaac Barré). Fervent parents hoping to inspire their children to fight for freedom began to add the name Wilkes to those, such as Oliver Cromwell, that they selected for their children. The most famous case of this is tragically familiar from a later stage in American history, in the name of John Wilkes Booth.

In this portrait of Wilkes he is flanked by Hercules and Minerva, exactly as in the image of James Otis Jr. on page 61. The two portraits served as covers for an almanac published in Boston, Wilkes in 1769 and Otis a year later. Clearly, the Americans saw Wilkes as involved in the same fight as they were.

Wilkes's English supporters could not wait to see him and show their support, but in May a riot broke out at one large gathering and several people were killed by government soldiers. Wilkes obtained a letter that suggested that the government itself had planned the attack, and he released it to the public. In early 1769 Parliament lashed back at Wilkes, calling his publication of the letter illegal and denying him his seat. He was furious and protested that the "sacred Rights of the People" had been "violated."

Now a clear confrontation between the voice of the people and the controlling hand of government was unfolding in England itself. Three times Wilkes was elected to Parliament, and three times he was barred from taking his place. The fourth time, he received 1,145 votes, his opponent 296, and yet again Parliament closed its doors to him. This was ominous news indeed for Americans who had no representation in Parliament, and whose streets were already occupied by English soldiers. A New Englander named William Palfrey saw the link clearly: "The fate of Wilkes and America must stand or fall together."

As the alarming confrontations between Boston and London escalated, the other colonies began to act. Refusing to buy English goods had worked once before, and the nonimportation movement was already under way in New England. In 1769 one after another the colonies joined in. The Philadelphia merchants, who had refused just a year earlier to sign on, did so, along with their competitors in New York. By the end of the year New Hampshire was the only colony that had not made a pact to stop trading in certain English goods. Working industriously throughout the year, the good women of Lancaster, Pennsylvania, produced 35,000 yards of cloth. The effects of these efforts, large and small, were dramatic, as the value of imports from England to the colonies fell from 2.1 million pounds, or 336 million modern dollars, to 1.3 million pounds (208 million dollars)

Boston July 31 1769

We the Subscribers Inhabitants of the Town of Boston being
desirous to concur with the Merchants and Traders of said Town
in their late laudable Agreement not to Import any of the
Manufactures of Great Britain, do hereby faithfully promise and
engage that we will abide by the following Resolutions

First.   That we will not, either by ourselves or any for or under us purchase
any Goods whatever from any Person or Persons who have or may
Import any of said Manufactures contrary to the Spirit of said
Agreement.

Secondly. That we will not, either by ourselves or any for or under us purchase
any of such Manufactures from any Factor or Factors who now do
or may hereafter expose the same for Sale.

Thirdly   We are determined to assist the said Merchants and Traders in
any further Measures that may be taken for the better carrying
their Resolutions into Execution.

In Testimony of all which we have hereunto set our
Names...   Mary Colley
           Susanah Grosden

           Wm Kennedy

           Rachell Manning
           Wm Whitfield
           John Hopkins sen
           Hammall & Brown
           Sand Johnson
           Jabl
           Ane Gillam

Eliz Clark
Eliza Nowell
Mary Wint
Elisa. Greenleaf
U. Frobisher
R. G. Franche
Elizabeth

Nonimportation as expressed by women signing agreements and pitching in at spinning bees can seem the most civilized of protests. But in Boston it could be as coercive as a hanging mob. For merchants did not really have a choice of whether or not to participate. Crowds gathered at the shops of anyone known to be breaking the boycott, and they held up signs accusing the owner of being an "IMPORTER." As one such merchant pointed out, it was "strange" that men protesting about having taxes imposed on them "should at the same time make laws" that they inflicted on others. A mob protesting against tyranny can still be a tyrannical mob.

Violent crowds intimidating merchants were not the only angry people in the city. English soldiers made a little extra money doing odd jobs, and they charged less than the Bostonians did. After a day of drinking and muttering, young men who were losing money roved the streets looking for soldiers to fight. Bristling behind their bayonets, the English were just as eager to shut them up.

On the moonlit night of March 5, 1770, a Boston boy insulted a soldier and got beaten up for it. It was not long before twenty men gathered to throw snowballs, ice, and more insults at the soldier. Someone ran off to start the local church bells ringing—the signal for a fire, which would quickly draw a larger crowd. The soldier's captain could see this happening and ordered the local guard, seven men, to bring things under control.

Opposite: *By signing this agreement, Bostonians showed their support for the nonimportation movement. As the date on the top shows, this was circulated in July 1769.* Inset: *Looking carefully at the agreement, the historian T. H. Breen found the faded signatures of women such as Elizabeth Clark, Elizabeth Nowell, Mary Hunt, Eliza Greenleaf, and Elizabeth (unreadable). By making this public declaration, and refusing to buy the imports, women became active participants in the resistance to the Townshend Acts.*
(MS. LARGE, IMAGE 652, COURTESY OF MASSACHUSETTS HISTORICAL SOCIETY)

When the guard reached the soldier, they spread into a line and loaded their muskets. This only angered the crowd, which pressed in on the soldiers. "Kill them!" someone shouted, while another ran along the line ticking off each gun, daring the soldiers to shoot.

Crack—a heavy piece of ice hit a soldier near the end of the line, he slipped, then shot. *Pause.* Every gun went off. Five men died, six were wounded, and Boston had its Massacre. The violence and intimidation that Adams used as a tool had its inevitable result. Angry, suspicious, fearful colonists, though, saw conspiracy at work: Soldiers had killed Wilkes's supporters in London and now Americans in the streets of Boston. The Massacre, they believed, was proof that evil was on the march. But that is not the end of the story.

Sam's cousin John was approached to defend the soldiers when they were brought up for trial. He took the unpopular case and spoke the truth: The crowd had been nothing but a "mob" that had provoked the soldier who first fired. What else could anyone expect him to have done, muse on the events like a philosopher? He urged the jury to see events as they had really transpired, not to satisfy their anger. For "it's of more importance to community, that innocence should be protected, than it is, that guilt should be punished." His clarity and moral certainty won the case.

If one part of the drive to oppose England was violence in the name of rights, another was upholding rights even when people thirsted for vengeance. Both forces were gaining strength in a Boston patrolled by English troops.

London had shown a willingness to send troops to assert its will. The colonies had shown an ability to act in concert to assert their rights. The idea of independence was no longer a child.

Paul Revere's famous engraving of the Boston Massacre was printed in the Boston Gazette, *alongside four black coffins with skulls and crossbones. Like Hogarth's "Gin Lane," this was art meant to inspire action and inflame passions. On both sides of the Atlantic partisans were mastering the skill of using images and the press to shape public opinion.*

HUNGER

The problem of long-distance management that Parliament experienced in its dealings with America was much worse for the East India Company, which was now ruling a part of India. As one astute writer put it, the company was governing "nations to which it takes a year to send orders." In early 1769 the company sent a three-man team to India to take charge. The ship carrying them disappeared without a trace—an apt outcome, for the jerry-built mixture of conquest, business, and governance that Clive left behind was about to collapse.

In May Madras was threatened by a powerful army led by the gifted leader Haidar Ali, and it was saved only by agreeing to his terms. India no longer seemed such a safe investment, and company stock crashed, dropping forty pounds in a month. That was ominous, but the really horrifying news came the following year.

Bengal was starving. When the usual September rains did not come, the rice fields turned as dry as straw. People had nothing to eat. As the only history of the famine tells it, "All through the stifling summer of 1770 the people went on dying. The husbandmen sold their cattle; they sold their implements of agriculture; they devoured their seed-grain; they sold their sons and daughters, till at length no buyer of children could be found; they ate the leaves of trees and the grass of the field; and in June, 1770, the Resident at the Durbar [a high English official] affirmed that the living were feeding on the dead."

The company was not responsible for the fickle rains. Though it was immensely fertile, Bengal starved whenever the clouds held back, and had suffered through terrible losses in Mogul times. But the company was accountable for its response. In the face of the Bengalis' anguish, the company hoarded rice to sell and increased the tax on land by 10 percent. While day-to-day tax collection was carried out by Indian officials who showed no compassion for the starving, the English were no better. Callous, greedy, and inexperienced at dealing with problems in Bengal, company officials did nothing as thousands, tens of thousands, hundreds of thousands, perhaps as many as 10 million people died. The effect of company rule was the death of one third of the rural population. This was not an epidemic like smallpox in North America, nor even the calculation of soldiers spreading disease among the Indians as a form of germ warfare. In Bengal millions died because the English, who now governed them, did not understand, did not care, and had not the least idea of how to help.

The horrors of Bengal were not ignored in England. More and more, influential people began to demand that the government regulate the East India Company. "We have outdone the Spaniard in Peru," the outspoken social commentator Horace Walpole said. "They were at least butchers on a religious principle, however diabolical their zeal. We have murdered, deposed, plundered, usurped—nay, what think you of the famine in Bengal in which three millions perished being caused by a monopoly of the servants of the East India Company?"

Critics had been carping at the company for decades, and now they had more ammunition. No business should be allowed to run a country. But for a government to tell a company what to do was heresy in England. Using language very much like that of the Americans protesting over taxes, stockholders called proposals to reform the company infringements on their liberty and property. At first, some Americans, such as those leading the Massachusetts protests, agreed.

In 1770 the clamor for regulating the company was not strong enough to move Parliament. But the issues being raised were directly related to the ones that brought troops to Boston. What was liberty? Freedom to enjoy one's property—what a man had built and earned—without having that stolen by a government. Freedom to think without being forced to mouth false phrases imposed by tyrants. Freedom to be a good person without having to fear that either mobs or nobles would silence you.

But did freedom to own property imply freedom to own people? To own countries? To let millions starve? To drive people off their land? Did freedom to think imply the right to reject the laws passed in Parliament? Did the right to be true to yourself include the right to intimidate others? To insult the king? On both sides of the Atlantic people felt that "liberty" was precious. But deciding what "liberty" meant threatened to tear the English Empire apart.

Townshend's half measures were failing on both sides, as America again boycotted English goods and the chaos and greed of the East India Company's rule in India were exposed. It was as if the colonies and the company were two icebergs growing closer and closer, and the English government were a boat in the middle spinning in ever-shrinking waters. One captain after another loudly exclaims that everything is under control, until the shadows cast by the icebergs cross and there is no space left at all.

CHAPTER 11

Tea

"A Design . . . to Enslave America"

Nonimportation was successful again. Faced with a disastrous loss of trade with the colonies, London backed down. All the Townshend taxes were ended, with just one exception—tea. Yet another minister, Lord North, was heading the government, and he was doing his best to ease tensions across the Atlantic. His efforts paid off. By the fall of 1770 even the Boston merchants decided to end their boycott, and in the three years between 1770 and 1773 English imports into the colonies nearly doubled over the previous three years. In turn, American exports to England quadrupled. Benjamin Franklin, it seemed, had been right in the first place. So long as good business sense prevailed, England and its American colonies could resolve their differences. White Americans, after all, now enjoyed the highest standard of living in the entire world. But despite this, many were uneasy—they didn't trust London, and wondered what threat to their rights and privileges would come next. They had a right to be concerned, for by this point London itself could no longer control events.

Alexander Fordyce was yet one more Scotsman seeking his fortune through the boom in the East India Company. One of those handsome, self-confident men who are particularly good at charming rich people into trusting him and lending him money, he also had a taste for high-stakes gambles. Fordyce married well, and he found backers to help him set up a bank in Scotland. But he was no careful investor handing out small loans to thrifty businesses. He bet far more money than the Ayr Bank actually had on East India Company stock.

In the summer of 1772 Fordyce guessed wrong on how the stock would perform (just when he assumed it would continue to decline, it rose slightly), and one fine day in June he realized that he was about to be ruined—he and his Ayr Bank owed a great deal more than they could ever repay. He grabbed whatever cash he could find and fled to France. Like perfectly aligned dominoes, banks throughout Scotland that had lent him money and also borrowed heavily to make risky investments collapsed. This set off one of the first true international banking crises. The cries of panic stretched down to England, over to Amsterdam, where there were many more speculators in company stock, from there through Europe, where kings and princes had come to depend on the Amsterdam stock market, across the Atlantic to the sugar plantations of the Caribbean, and not long after to the American colonies.

Virginia planters discovered to their horror that their Scottish bankers were demanding rapid payment of all outstanding debts, even if the planters

The "macaroni gambler"—in other words, the fashionable, well-dressed banker who has grabbed his money and left his fellow Scots holding the bill—shown here is Alexander Fordyce. He set in motion the chain reaction that made the American Revolution inevitable.

had to auction off their fine homes and sell their gangs of slaves to meet their obligations. Nothing was more humiliating, or infuriating, to the proud squires. The bankruptcies set off by Fordyce's gamble on company stock spread like a disease throughout Virginia.

Every ruined, angry squire, every frightened neighbor seeing auction signs going up on mansions owned by leading families, had one more reason to distrust and detest England, and one more reason to yearn for independence. They kept offering us loans, the Virginians protested, so of course we spent more—they were setting us up, and now we've lost everything. We need to be free of their control. A very few planters may have argued for independence simply to avoid paying their debts, but most were just miserable and filled with blame. The angrier they became, the more they echoed the views of thoughtful leaders such as George Washington and John Adams, who had already decided that a complete break with England was inevitable.

George Washington had come to this realization as early as 1769, when Virginia was considering joining the nonimportation movement. Writing to his neighbor George Mason, he showed his weary frustration with "our lordly masters in Great Britain." By this time Washington was certain London would stop at nothing less than destroying American freedom. Faced with that dark and unrelenting plan, he believed that "no man should scruple or hesitate a moment to use a-ms [arms]."

Washington's early losses in battle had made him a more careful, cautious soldier. In the coming war one of his greatest strengths would be avoiding battles he could not win. But he was proud, confident, and now sure that the time for fighting was near. What Washington wrote was just beneath the surface for many Americans. All it would take for that view to be expressed was one more clear sign of what John Adams had already called "a direct and formal design . . . to enslave America." London soon obliged.

COLLAPSE

Just as banks were scrambling to stay afloat in the wake of the Fordyce crisis, the East India Company ran out of cash. Clive had been much too optimistic about how profitable it would be to run Bengal, and that was before the famine. Between the sliding profits from Bengal and declining sales of Indian products in an England that was in the midst of a cascade of bank failures, the company simply could not pay its bills. To begin with, it could not cover the 400,000-pound annual payment it had promised to the government in Townshend's day. The already nervous Bank of England refused to extend new credit. Debts piled up upon debts, and by the following fall the company owed over 1.3 million pounds, or 208 million dollars. Some of the company directors did not want anyone to know this, since they owned stock that would crash once the news became public. There was just one way for them to at best cover up the problem, and at least ensure that the company would not go bankrupt itself: turn to the government for a loan.

It will certainly sound strange, but the best way to picture this crucial moment in English and American history is through one of the great scenes in Italian opera. In Giacomo Puccini's *Tosca*, Floria Tosca is a singer whose lover has been captured by a villain—who is himself in love with the singer. Tosca goes to the evil Baron Scarpia and asks him what it will take to free the man she loves. How much? What is the price? Of course Scarpia wants her, and she stabs him to death instead—this is Italian opera, after all. Still, Tosca's stark question is exactly what the East India Company asked the English government: "What is the price?" "What do we have to give up in order to survive?"

Two answers came easily: control of India and reform of the company. In 1773 the English government, under Lord North, proposed a Regulating Bill, lending the company money but ending its independence. Slowly but surely, from this moment on, the company was forced to cede its authority in India to the government, and to revise its rules to prevent the frenzied buying and selling of its stock. But even as Lord North negotiated with the company over how much power it would give up, it became clear that there was also another kind of price to be paid.

Humanitarians in England had been disturbed by the famine. Their outrage at the East India Company was stoked by two new and widely promoted exposés about its practices in India. Since his very first fight with Clive, Sulivan had learned how to use newspapers and books to influence public opinion in very much the same ways employed by Sam Adams. These books were calculated attacks, not balanced accounts—one of the authors had been deeply involved with John Johnstone in unscrupulous business practices. But an angry public was not looking for sober history and academic debate. They wanted villains to blame.

Once the true condition of the company leaked out, the stock crashed and many investors were ruined. Those stockholders were furious to learn that some of the directors who were hiding the facts had tried to sell their own holdings before the price dropped. Suddenly, the company that had made so many investors rich seemed evil, and people wanted the devil behind it to be named and punished.

In yet another turn of their endless struggle, Sulivan was once again the dominant power in the East India Company, and Clive the outsider. Sulivan had lost a fortune in the stock crash and was not among the corrupt directors. His primary goal was power, not wealth. He, and Clive's enemies in Parliament, especially the vindictive Johnstone brothers, realized that this was their golden opportunity. While one committee in Parliament considered Lord North's bill to lend the company money, another was organized to expose its sins. This second committee was not really interested in a dispassionate study of company behavior. Led by George Johnstone, it was out to destroy Lord Clive, to take away his annual payment, and to make him the scapegoat for everything that had gone wrong.

When he came before the committee, Clive held Parliament spellbound for two hours. He insisted that it was his "duty to the public" to challenge the men who were robbing India and undermining the company, no matter how many enemies he made. This was true, though it left an obvious question: What about his own Indian fortune? For the moment, he spoke with such confidence and eloquence that he did not have to give an answer. But the interlude did not last.

Even as Parliament continued to work out the details of the bailout of the East India Company, Colonel John Burgoyne, an ambitious politician, saw an opportunity to make a name for himself. He organized another Parliamentary committee that would meet in secret to continue the investigation of the company and, especially, of Clive. At George Johnstone's urging they reviewed Clive's behavior as far back as 1757, even before Plassey. That meant he had to answer not only for his special annual fee but even for his deception of Omichand, the Indian merchant who had helped him with Mir Jafar.

Step by step, Clive was forced to defend every deal, every agreement, every decision he had made in India. This was at times embarrassing, and when the public learned of things like the forged signature, Clive was attacked not only in words but in sneering cartoons. Rumor had it that people shuddered when they passed one of his lavish homes. And yet Clive actually managed to explain his actions, and to come across as a flawed but appealing person. Horace Walpole, no friend of Clive's, was impressed: "He shone eminently as a real great man, who had done great things."

Right: *Clive, kneeling on the right and facing out, and one of the directors of the East India Company, are offering moneybags to Lord North, begging him to protect them. In the background Lord Bute (his feathered tam-o'-shanter identifies him as Scottish) chases off justice. Satires like this both reflected and stimulated public outrage at the company and Clive.*

(BM SAT 5111, COURTESY THE BRITISH MUSEUM)

Opposite page, left: *In this satire George Johnstone faces the directors of the East India Company, using one director, Sir George Colebrooke, as a kind of puppet. The reading public in England and America was angry and watching the fights in both Parliament and the East India Company very closely.*

(BM SAT 5100, COURTESY THE BRITISH MUSEUM)

Opposite page, right: *Omichand was the merchant/go-between Clive had fooled in India, and he was said to have been so crushed that he soon died. This cartoon has Omichand's ghost looming up to haunt a horrified Clive.*

(BM SAT 5101, COURTESY THE BRITISH MUSEUM)

Neither Burgoyne nor the vengeful press was satisfied, and the colonel suggested that any money Parliament gave to the company be linked with penalties against Clive. Isaac Barré was allied with Sulivan and against Clive, and he took the opportunity to contrast his memory of the great, almost saintly James Wolfe with this man who turned his victories into private gain. On May 10, 1773, Parliament passed three motions Burgoyne had proposed that laid the groundwork for taking back Clive's entire fortune. Nine days later they met again, to decide his fate.

Clive always excelled in battle, and he responded well to the challenge. He walked his fellow members of Parliament through the history of his wars in India, being careful to seem modest and to praise others. By recounting his conquests in India, though, Clive was quietly challenging men grown rich on his courage to remember the source of their good fortune. Then he changed tone, suggesting that he would not mind losing everything, living as modestly as his father had before his son set out for India, so long as he was true to himself. Speaking as a man willing to be stripped of everything he had earned, he turned the spotlight back on his accusers: Could they really punish him for gifts he had received sixteen years earlier? "I have only one thing more," he said in his brilliant conclusion, "that is a humble request to the House, I make it not for myself, but for them, the request is this, when they come to decide upon my honor, they will not forget their own."

Could they really ruin a man who had done so much for his country, especially when none of them had clean hands? Everyone knew how John Johnstone, for example, had extorted his fortune in India. What right did he and his brothers have to condemn Clive?

Parliament was made up of factions voting for their own interests. But they were also men who listened to and could be swayed by powerful speeches. Clive's words won him support, though it was not clear if that was enough. Two days later, on May 21, the issue came to a vote. Would the man who had given Bengal to the East India Company, and in that way started the British Empire, lose everything?

On the fateful night, Clive spoke for just a few minutes, urging the members to "leave me my honor, take away my fortune." Whether it was pure theater or true emotion, he then left before tears spilled out of his eyes. He returned to his London home to sit with his wife and wait. Clive's enemies were unrelenting, which began to disturb those who had been moved by his words. One admiral had a sense that what had been a fair hearing was turning into a travesty. A notorious low point of English justice had come one hundred seventy years earlier, when King James I arranged a show trial to demonstrate his power and to eliminate a man he disliked. Admiral Charles Saunders objected that Clive was being treated by Parliament with exactly the same perversion of law as James I had shown to Sir Walter Ralegh when he was tried for treason in 1603. The debate went on for hour after hour, until night turned into early morning.

At five in the morning the clattering of horses' hooves announced the arrival of a carriage at Clive's home. An ally of Clive's entered the drawing room and gave the verdict: An hour earlier Parliament had voted to leave his fortune untouched and, instead, commend him for the great services he had performed for England.

If you are a romantic who likes big-spirited, if flawed, leaders, Clive finally got his due, and it was only appropriate that his scheming enemies were left to gnash their teeth. If you are a cynic, then the outcome shows how a person who has enough wealth, influence, and theatrical skill can always protect himself. But even cynics would probably not have anticipated the ultimate outcome of the hearing.

Clive never completely recovered from his last collapse in India. Even though he had cleared his name and saved his fortune, he had no more role to play. The government was taking over India, and he could not control the East India Company. Worse yet, after devoting his life to lifting himself and his family out of its decline, after buying his way into Parliament, becoming a lord, even winning an empire, he had been treated as a common "sheep

Painted a year before Clive's death, Edward Penny's image records a moment when Clive accepted money from Mir Jafar to give out to English military widows and invalids. This is the image in which he most resembles George Washington.   (FOSTER 91, COURTESY THE BRITISH LIBRARY)

stealer" in front of the very men he had tried to impress. After the ordeal of being tried in front of Parliament, the end that had loomed in his mind ever since his first days in Madras became compelling. On November 22, 1774, Robert, Lord Clive, the hero of Plassey, took his own life.

Clive was driven to suicide by his own demons—perhaps nothing could have saved him from himself. But his dramatic death was also a kind of final judgment of the first phase of English expansion in India. A radical named Thomas Paine saw the suicide as the only proper end for such an evil man,

Charles Willson Peale painted this second portrait of George Washington in 1790.
(ACCESSION NO. 1867.299 COLLECTION OF THE NEW-YORK HISTORICAL SOCIETY)

and as a moral indictment of England itself for profiting from his victories. Famine-ravaged India, he wrote, was a monument to the cruelty of Christian Europe.

GEORGE WASHINGTON AND ROBERT CLIVE

In certain portraits Robert Clive looks a great deal like a puffy version of George Washington. Clive once remarked that he was sure the American colonists would win their independence, and would eventually even take over all of South America. And yet, at least according to one rumor, there had been serious talk of sending him over to America to lead the English forces against the colonists. That would have made him and Washington direct opponents. His suicide prevented that contest from taking place.

Though Clive and Washington did not meet in battle, it does make sense to compare them—to treat them as strange twins, whose differences are as revealing as their similarities.

Washington was intensely proud of his virtue and self-control. He would never have passed a forged document, or taken a bribe that would allow people to speak of him as corrupt. From his boyhood on, he was determined to improve himself, but never at the sacrifice of his integrity. Reputation—how people saw him and spoke of him—was as important as winning battles or making money. Once it became clear to him that America must be independent, he treated his country the way he had treated himself: with discipline, ambition, and a firm moral compass.

Clive was a kind of reverse Washington: He was the creator, the father, of British India. He was proud of what he accomplished, and thought his critics were hypocrites who simply did not understand conditions in India. Indeed, many of Clive's enemies were snobs who disliked him for being self-made, an outsider, even as they bought stock in the East India Company. Others were latecomers frustrated by his reforms when it became their turn to bring fortunes home from India. His suicide was in part a judgment on the English society that wanted the results of his energy and drive, but without accepting him.

You could say that Washington fought against England because he did not want to become a Clive—he refused to remain part of a country that had the kind of social barriers that would frustrate its greatest general while also eagerly profiting from his victories. But the differences between the two men were not only a matter of where they lived.

Clive was a man of his times. He had immense energy and drive but a fatal lack of moral sense. That was very much like the Parliament, and the England, of his day. America was no better, and the land hunger of the Americans, including Washington, was quite similar to the greed of the East India Company men in India. But the two leaders left behind completely different legacies. That is because Washington went beyond merely reflecting the standards of the world around him and crafted himself into a figure that stood for principles of good government, responsible leadership, and public service. As a result, Washington helped to build an independent nation, while the India Clive helped to shape was characterized by military conquest and mismanagement, English fortunes and Bengali famine.

More pragmatically, Clive's dramatic end was a sign that the time for self-made generals fighting epic battles was ending; government officers and bureaucrats would take over. Men very much like the customs officers and tax collectors whom Sam Adams detested became the rulers of India.

After much discussion and negotiation with the company, Lord North's Regulating Act became law on June 21, 1773. It offered the company a loan of 1.4 million pounds, 224 million modern dollars, in exchange for reforms in the firm, and new government control in India.

North saved the East India Company. But how could the company ever repay the government? To a historian the answer to this question is almost diabolically perfect: It is like the one single, exquisitely crafted keystone that holds together an arch, bonding the two sides into a single curve. For it is here, at this critical juncture, that the story of Clive and Siraj, of Sulivan and the Johnstones, joins the more familiar narrative of American history.

The company had one great asset that had nothing to do with India: warehouses filled with 18,000,000 pounds (by weight) of Chinese tea. Someone calculated that if the company lowered the price of tea below what smugglers charged, sold the majority of it far enough away from the country that it could not be shipped back and resold, and eliminated the tax the company usually paid for shipping tea out of England, the company could make the nice round sum of 1,425,000 pounds—228 million dollars—just enough to repay the government and balance the company's books, with a bit to spare. By now the American colonies were drinking as much tea as all of England, though half or more was smuggled in and produced no revenue for the crown. Selling cheap tea to the colonies was the perfect solution to the crisis created by the failure of the East India Company.

There was just one problem. One Townshend duty still remained, and it was placed on tea. Everyone knew that the small amount of revenue the tax would generate was insignificant. So why not remove it? One member of Parliament even warned North directly: "I tell the Noble Lord now, if he don't take off the duty they won't take the tea." But that last meaningless fee carried with it the entire principle that Grenville, and Townshend, and Pitt, and Rockingham, and now North were determined to assert: Parliament could set any rules for the colonies that it chose. Giving in to the colonists would be like turning India back over to the East India Company. London was determined to exert control to the very edges of its empire. On May 10, 1773, knowing that the Regulating Act was about to become law, Parliament passed the Tea Act, sending low-priced company tea to America with its Townshend duty intact.

In the fall of 1773, 2,000 chests carrying 600,000 pounds of East India Company tea were loaded into ships headed for New York, Charleston, Philadelphia, and Boston—600,000 pounds of salvation for the embattled company; 600,000 pounds of the might of England, her proud Parliament, her glorious king; 600,000 pounds of fuel for the fire of revolution.

CHAPTER 12

Intolerable

ACTION

It is nearly six in the evening, Thursday, December 16, 1773, and a cold rain is falling in Boston. Five thousand people from throughout Massachusetts have spent much of the day squeezed into the hard wooden benches and galleries of the Old South Church. They know that each minute that passes brings them closer to the most important decision they have ever faced.

The *Dartmouth*, carrying company tea, arrived in port nineteen days earlier. Thomas Hutchinson, who is now the governor, has insisted that he will not let the ship return its cargo to England. He is right—that would be illegal. But the governors of other colonies will do it anyway. Hutchinson is being adamant because he knows he has the Sons of Liberty in a trap. Once the tea crossed the invisible line in the water marking the beginning of Boston Harbor, it could not be sold without paying the duty. And, by law, if a ship carrying tea does not unload its cargo within twenty days, the boxes will be seized and held by the governor. The ship cannot sail: Hutchinson and the English navy will see to that. The tea will not be unloaded: The Sons of Liberty own the docks. But tomorrow the governor will take control of it. He can then take his time to find a buyer who will pay the Townshend tax, and the principle that Parliament can tax as it chooses will be reinforced. Just one more day and Hutchinson wins.

The day's meeting has been part discussion, part trial, as the crowd has kept pushing at Francis Rotch, owner of the Dartmouth, *to find a solution. They have insisted that he defy the governor and send the ship back to London; they have even sent him to Hutchinson's country home to make a last plea. But now he is back, with the final word.*

The darkness of the December evening is barely eased by a few candles. Everyone is edgy from the heat of too many bodies pressed too close together, tense, expectant. Rotch speaks: The governor will not budge. The air crackles with the hostility of the crowd, people yell for "a mob," "a mob," as if they could crush the owner, his ship, and his tea all at once. But then Sam Adams rises, and sadly, as if resigned, says there is nothing more that can be done.

Someone yells out a war whoop and then, "The Mohawks are come." The screams are so loud, they can be heard blocks away, and suddenly thousands of men are pouring out of the church doors and down toward the docks. Adams's words are a code, the prearranged signal his men are waiting to hear. The pressure-cooker day of tension in the church has been merely a prelude for the real action, under the cover of night.

Samuel Adams, as painted by John Singleton Copley. The most popular portrait painter in America, Copley painted Adams around 1770. Ironically, Copley married into a family that imported tea from England. On December 16, 1773, with his father-in-law's tea sitting in Boston Harbor, Copley was at the heart of the heated discussions, desperately hoping to find a solution to the crisis. He left shortly after the Boston Tea Party and never returned to America.

(NATIONAL ARCHIVES AND RECORDS ADMINISTRATION)

There are by now three boats in the harbor carrying a total of 90,000 pounds by weight of company tea, worth nearly 1.5 million modern dollars. Lightly disguised and painted as Indians, the well-organized wrecking crews have lanterns and axes, and they split up into teams, each with its own captain. For three hours they systematically find, lift, hack open, and dump the chests of tea into the harbor, while a large crowd watches from the shore.

* * *

Accounts of the Tea Party stress the size of the crowd that watched the event. This picture is from the same 1784 book as the illustration of the Stamp Act riots on page 98. Both blacks and whites worked near the docks and were likely to have gathered to watch the destruction of the tea. (LIBRARY OF CONGRESS)

A shoemaker who joined in the action later recalled how efficient they were: "We were ordered by our commander to open the hatches, and take out all the chests of tea and throw them overboard, and we immediately proceeded to execute his orders; first cutting and splitting the chests with our tomahawks, so as thoroughly to expose them to the effects of the water. In about three hours from the time we went on board, we had thus broken and thrown overboard every tea chest to be found in the ship; while those in the other ships were disposing of the tea in the same way, at the same time."

John Adams immediately recognized that the shattered boxes his cousin's men had cast into the harbor were an unmistakable sign that they were all on a new road. "The destruction of the tea is so bold, so daring, so firm, intrepid, and inflexible . . . I cannot but consider it as an epocha [turning point moment] in history."

REACTION

By late January 1774 news of the Boston Tea Party had reached London. The days of compromise and debate were over. England was determined to establish beyond the slightest doubt that the colonies were under its rule. First, the port of Boston must be closed, sealed to all but necessary trade in food and fuel, until the company was fully compensated for the 90,000 pounds of tea. Even Isaac Barré thought this was fair and just.

Parliament did not stop there. For the first time in the history of British North America, it insisted that the charter for a colony be changed and local control reduced. Massachusetts, like the company territories in India, must now be under the king's supervision. Another bill insisted that English troops be allowed to stay in private homes. Finally, though it was not a response to the Tea Party, Parliament proposed—and the king signed—one last measure dealing with North America. The Quebec Act extended the borders of Canada down to the Ohio River, and gave this territory a government that was entirely alien to the English colonies: Trials would not be by jury, and the Catholic Church would continue to have great influence. This was the very land that land-speculation firms such as the Ohio Company and the Loyal Land Company had hoped to buy and sell, and London was now taking it completely out of their control.

In what the colonists soon called the Intolerable Acts, Parliament suc-

This cartoon shows the fear the Quebec Act inspired: four bishops from the Church of England celebrate the act, while the evil Lord Bute sets them dancing with his bagpipes, Lord North approves, and the devil supervises.   (LIBRARY OF CONGRESS)

ceeded in fulfilling not merely the worst fears of the conspiracy theorists, but also the dark prophecies that had been circulating since the days of the English Civil War 130 years earlier. As Jefferson put it, this was proof of "a deliberate and systematical plan of reducing us to slavery." Washington agreed that London was "endeavoring by every piece of art and despotism to fix the shackles of slavery upon us." After all, the Quebec Act actually imposed "popery" in Canada. This was actually a reasonable response to the fact that most of the people in what had once been New France were Catholics. But to suspicious Americans it was a forecast of the loss of rights and imposition of an alien faith that London had in mind for them. A Baptist preacher named John Allen, who had recently left England for America, warned that the government intended to turn the colonists into "spiritless SLAVES" as they had been "in the reign of the *Stuarts*."

One more time the sense of dire threat from London drew the colonists together. By September every colony except Georgia had agreed to send representatives to the First Continental Congress, meeting in Philadelphia. Twenty years earlier, the threat of war had led to Franklin's first proposal for joint action among the colonies, the Albany Plan. Nine years earlier, in 1765, nine colonies had gathered in the Stamp Act Congress. Each decade the colonies were knit more closely together and grew more firm in their resolve. Now the meeting would hear from people who had already decided that a break from England must come: from Massachusetts, John and Sam Adams; from Virginia, George Washington, Patrick Henry, and the equally radical Richard Henry Lee. But the congress also heard from conservatives, such as Pennsylvania's Joseph Galloway, an articulate and influential man who had at one time been Franklin's most important political ally.

The congress listened to all, and reaffirmed its loyalty to the king but rejected any right of Parliament to regulate the internal affairs within the borders of the colonies. It resolved not only to disobey the Intolerable Acts but to begin to form militias, and to establish a firm boycott of all English goods. One more time, Americans were urged to unite by being frugal and industrious and by rejecting "extravagance and dissipation, especially horse-racing, and all kinds of gaming, cock-fighting, exhibitions of shews [shows], plays, and other expensive diversions and entertainments."

By late fall the men who would later lead the Revolution knew it was coming. They had met and begun the process of defining, for themselves and for all the colonies, what they believed in, what they would fight for, and what they wanted to create on their shared soil. But many leading Americans, such as Galloway and the influential John Dickinson, did not share their vision. And for all their idealism there was the question about whom the leaders represented. It took a man who had just arrived from England to ensure that all Americans truly believed in, and understood, the coming conflict.

CHAPTER 13

Common Sense

"An Asylum for Mankind"

Benjamin Franklin was in London when the ministers developed the Intolerable Acts. While there, he met a man who was eager to emigrate to America. Tom Paine's second marriage had failed, and he had also fumbled a succession of jobs. Nevertheless, Franklin liked him and gave him a letter of introduction. Paine arrived in America in 1774 and soon found a job working on the new *Pennsylvania Magazine,* whose first issue appeared on January 1, 1775. He served as both editor and author. As a result, a man who could speak with the passion that had driven England's radicals ever since their civil war was now publishing in America to Americans.

Paine was a Quaker, and he shared the moral passion of the movement's founders. One of the first attention-getting pieces he wrote for *Pennsylvania*

Thomas Paine—an engraving based on a portrait painted from life.   (LIBRARY OF CONGRESS)

asked of Americans, "with what consistency, or decency [can] they complain so loudly of attempts to enslave them, while they hold so many hundred thousands in slavery." If Americans hated slavery, if they were claiming to be more moral than their English oppressors, he asked, how could they hold slaves themselves? In the face of the agonies and confusions of people like Jefferson and Washington, Paine was absolutely clear.

Paine's Quaker background gave him more than just moral clarity. It was through groups like the Quakers that some of the most extreme views of the English Civil War were kept alive. Debating with Oliver Cromwell in 1647, Leveller leaders had demanded that every Englishman with some property have a say in the government. *Every man.* Paine burned with that same sense of the government belonging to all the people. It was the most fundamental right, and rules that kept power in the hands of lords, or kings, or any small group, were simply wrong.

As a poor young man scrambling to make his way in London, Paine was exactly the sort of person who believed in and supported John Wilkes. He had witnessed Wilkes being excluded from Parliament time after time. He knew that Parliament could trample on the rights of people in England, so it certainly could not be trusted in America.

A Quaker, a firebrand in the Leveller tradition, a Londoner who knew the saga of John Wilkes intimately, Paine brought with him the purest fire of English radicalism. But even more than that, having lived in the London streets amidst the poor, the destroyed victims of gin, of prostitution, of a society only too willing to let its weakest die, he brought with him the clarity of rage and contempt. Any words about English law, English liberty, English rights were, to him, merely lies—lies used to disguise a diseased society.

Tom Paine came to America to live, but when he wrote for Americans, it was as someone who knew in his bones the misery of English life. In 1775, as the first clashes of the war played out and the Americans began to face the reality of battling the most powerful nation on earth, Dr. Benjamin Rush— an important Philadelphia doctor and antislavery campaigner—suggested that Paine produce a pamphlet advocating independence. Paine thought to call his writing *Plain Truth*. He would tell wavering Americans the simple, clear truth about England, so that they could have the courage to break free. But Rush convinced him to change the title to *Common Sense*. And it was under that title that Paine's words made history.

Common Sense was published on January 9, 1776. It spoke directly, vividly, and passionately to Americans about their destiny: "The cause of America," it urged, "is in a great measure the cause of all mankind." That was because America had, at this precise moment, the unique opportunity to undo the errors of history and give government back to the people.

In 1584, when Sir Walter Ralegh first sent Philip Amadas, Arthur Barlowe, and their men to the Americas, they reported that the natives enjoyed almost perfect lives. Paine asked his readers to imagine what kind of government the very first settlers of an uninhabited land must have had. He did not specifically refer to Barlowe's report, so the issue of American Indians did not arise. But for his American readers it must have been obvious that he was talking about the New World. As Paine explained, free people in a new land would band together only to face common dangers and to help those in need. When John Winthrop wrote about his vision of the Massachusetts Bay Colony he was coming to lead, it was in similar terms. Without going over any one actual history, Paine was giving his readers a picture of the pageant of their past.

According to Paine, only when there are too many people, and they are too spread out across the land, will they need to elect representatives to speak for them. Government, then, is necessary solely because it offers people more than they can create individually, and because not everyone in the world will be a good neighbor, a good friend. Why, then, could anyone possibly want to have a king—a person standing above the agreements of the people? England had faced this problem once, and Charles I had paid with his head. Since then, English kings have been "more subtle—not more just." Having reminded his readers of a version of the history of the colonies, Paine was now leading them back through England's bloody past. Kings were not better than other men, they were simply the "principal ruffian of some restless gang" that had the good fortune to win power. Here was the voice of the Levellers finally speaking to people ready to hear their message.

If kings were a perversion of government, what of aristocracy? Since "all men" were "originally equals," it was ridiculous to let anyone inherit power over others. Paine was laying out the simple yet startling principle that Jefferson would echo in the opening lines of the Declaration of Independence six months later: "all men are created equal."

Paine knew that even though they wanted England to grant the colonies more rights, many of his readers were against fighting a war of independence. Hadn't England been their good, nurturing parent? No. For neither were all Americans of English background, nor had England been a good home. "This new world hath been the asylum for the persecuted lovers of civil and religious liberty from *every part* of Europe. Hither have they fled, not from the tender embraces of the mother, but from the cruelty of the monster." Like the rest of Europe, England was a cruel monster to its children, a tyrant. No sane person would want to remain attached to such parents.

Though Paine had been in America for a very short time, where he lived mattered. In Pennsylvania the politics, religious beliefs, even the languages spoken were very different from those of either the New England Puritans or the Virginia planters. There were German farmers, Scotch-Irish backwoodsmen, enslaved and free blacks, as well as English, Irish, and Welsh; there were Quakers, Presbyterians, Lutherans, Mennonites, and Jews, American Indians, as well as Anglicans. Though the groups often clashed, Pennsylvania was not a colony that could imagine it was fulfilling any one group's prophecies. Like its neighbor New York, which had its own mixture of English, Dutch, French, Brazilian, Portuguese, American Indian, and enslaved and free black peoples, Pennsylvania society was dominated by commerce more than by religion. When Paine rejected the idea that England was America's mother, he was describing the world outside his window. And while Boston and Virginia deserve credit for crystallizing the grand ideas of the Revolution, the polyglot lives of people in the Middle Atlantic colonies were actually a better prediction of what the new nation would look like.

America, Paine urged, must seize its moment. Any step backward into a revised form of union with England would bring disaster. And this would not just be a failure for the colonists, it would be a failure for all humanity. In his most dramatic writing, Paine addressed his readers as if he were an orator, a minister, and gave them their sacred charge: "O ye that love mankind! Ye that dare oppose, not only the tyranny, but the tyrant, stand forth! Every spot of the old world is overrun with oppression. Freedom hath been hunted round the globe. Asia, and Africa, have long expelled her—Europe regards her like a stranger, and England hath given her warning to depart. O! receive the fugitive, and prepare in time an asylum for mankind."

America must fight for its independence not merely to protect the liberties of the colonists but to protect liberty itself for all human beings.

MAKING A NATION

Dickinson's "Letters" had swept across the colonies, helping to focus the opposition to the stamp tax. But *Common Sense* sold one hundred times as many copies in a single year as the "Letters" had sold in the eight years since they were first published. Unlike Dickinson, Paine was not making a lawyer's argument. His passionate words were so clear, so devastating, so commonsensical that he was no longer debating—he simply made other views look ridiculous. That very fire alienated conservatives. Thinking, perhaps, of erudite Bostonians, John Adams guessed that as many people were offended by it as agreed with it. But even if some Americans disliked it, they read it. And in that way *Common Sense* became the bible of the Revolution—the one text that all literate Americans read.

The first anonymous copies of Paine's book were printed in Philadelphia. Within weeks it had spread across the country and sold somewhere between 100,000 and 150,000 copies. The book was distributed throughout the colonies in much the same way as e-mails move through the Internet. One printer would issue a copy, another would see it and bring out his own, a newspaper would reprint it, which would pass it along to a third printer. According to a source in Philadelphia, even people who could not read were asking to have it read to them, and Washington requested that it be read to his soldiers. *Common Sense* was like a color spreading across a map, highlighting all the means of communication that could serve to unite the people. Read and, in effect, downloaded by one shop after another, Paine's book established beyond all doubt that the colonies were now one entity, not thirteen squabbling children looking to a parent for approval.

Historians speak of all the readers of any one book as an imaginary community: Wherever each reader is in physical reality, he or she also lives in the world of that book. Everyone who has read the Bible, for example, has at least that in common with a large community of readers all around the world. *Common Sense* created the imaginary community of a new, free, independent America.

COMMON SENSE,

ADDRESSED TO THE

INHABITANTS

OF

AMERICA,

On the following interesting

SUBJECTS.

I. Of the Origin and Design of Government in general, with concise Remarks on the English Constitution.

II. Of Monarchy and Hereditary Succession.

III. Thoughts on the present State of American Affairs.

IV. Of the present Ability of America, with some miscellaneous Reflections.

Man knows no Master save creating HEAVEN,
Or those whom choice and common good ordain.
THOMSON.

PHILADELPHIA Printed:

NEW-YORK, Reprinted and Sold, by JOHN ANDERSON, the Corner of Beekman's-Slip.

What was the change in the minds of the people John Adams called the real Revolution? What was this child that had grown in the speeches of New England lawyers, in the resolutions of Virginia planters, in the hatchets and tar buckets of Boston mobs, in the rifles and skins of backcountry hunters, in the sayings and experiments of Benjamin Franklin, in the markets of New York and Philadelphia, in the words of Tom Paine? It was a feeling of ownership—what I build is mine; it was a sense of right—what I think is for me to decide; it was a sense of opportunity to do good and to live righteously. Once a person experienced this feeling of autonomy, he or she knew that nothing was more precious.

Living in the new land gave people a taste, a feeling, for being independent. That deep sense opened a wedge, a sliver of space, between life as they experienced it and the assumptions of the vast majority of other people on Earth. It was this invisible gap, this shift, that the succession of English lords and members of Parliament could not see, could not appreciate, could not understand. Every time these legislators passed laws that were blind to the growing sense of independence that had become fundamental to some Americans, the colonists saw a pattern. As the English could not appreciate independence, they must be determined to crush it, they must want to eradicate it.

The colonists were wrong. The English did not so much have a plot to destroy their independence as they could not understand what it was. From London the Americans' insistence on having their own judgment, making

Opposite: *This edition of* Common Sense *was published in New York, but it also notes original publication in Philadelphia—this is Internet-like transmission of information in action.*
(ACCESSION NO. 76764D COLLECTION OF THE NEW-YORK HISTORICAL SOCIETY)

their own rules, seemed to be immaturity, as it sometimes was; greed, as was often the case; selfishness, certainly so; hypocrisy, unquestionably. London was right in all of its criticisms. But because it did not savor independence for its own people, it could not understand what the Americans were carping about. As James Otis had long ago said, if London felt it was right in depriving the colonists of a vote in Parliament because it also gave no voice to the people of Manchester, the answer was to enfranchise Manchester, not to deny the colonists. London responded with anger, seeking to crush impertinence, which only confirmed Americans' sense that a conspiracy had been afoot all along.

This incomprehension was particularly evident to one set of Paine's readers: people who had recently immigrated to America. In the seventy-five years since 1700 the population of the colonies had increased almost ninefold, from 250,000 to 2,150,000. This rise in population had been most dramatic in the past decade, when the number of people in the colonies increased 35 percent. People who had chosen to leave Europe and come to America knew why they had done so. When Paine wrote of the monstrosities of royalty and nobility, and of the opportunity Americans had to take a different, better, path, he was speaking to those who had come to similar decisions in their own lives. Ironically, the fact that he himself was a recent immigrant who knew the flaws of Europe better than the realities of America allowed him to speak all the more forcefully to many of his readers.

With the publication of Paine's book, the Revolution in the minds of Americans was complete. Helped by John Adams and Benjamin Franklin, Jefferson officially declared that to be so on July 4, 1776. But the global interconnections that had led to that point continued to shape the road to true independence, and beyond.

* * *

In 1777 John Burgoyne, who had tried to take away Clive's fortune, surrendered to the Americans at Saratoga, New York. Winning that series of battles was a crucial turning point in the war, because it gave the French confidence that the Americans could win. After that, through the astute diplomacy of Benjamin Franklin and the less subtle but indefatigable efforts of John Adams, the government of the French king supplied the money

This famous painting by John Trumbull shows the signing of the Declaration, with Jefferson towering at dead center, Adams behind him with his hand on his hip, and Franklin to his left.
(NATIONAL ARCHIVES AND RECORDS ADMINISTRATION)

Franklin enjoyed being in France. As this painting shows, he was very comfortable flirting with the rather forward Frenchwomen.   (NATIONAL ARCHIVES AND RECORDS ADMINISTRATION)

America needed to continue the fight. And when on October 19, 1781, Washington finally cornered his opponent, Lord Cornwallis, in Yorktown, Virginia, it was the ships of the French navy that sealed the trap.

Fighting for England against France, Washington had set off the Seven Years' War. Now, twenty-eight years later, as the leader of the Americans, Washington and the French combined to beat the English. That is just one way in which the international connections that shaped the path to the American Revolution continued to play out around the world. For even after the Revolution the global drama of America, England, India, and empire continued to unfold.

Hemmed in by the French navy, the English surrender to the Americans.

CHAPTER 14

Revolutions

THE JEWEL IN THE CROWN

It is January 1877, just over a century after Paine's book and Jefferson's Declaration. A grand ceremony is being held in London. Four hundred princes have traveled from India to attend; they are flanked by 15,000 soldiers in uniform. All have gathered to celebrate the official declaration that Queen Victoria is now the Empress of India. The event has been staged and masterminded by her prime minister, Benjamin Disraeli. As he has told his queen, India is the jewel in her crown. Disraeli's phrase exactly echoes what Grenville said of America as he left office in 1765. Much has happened in the century to cause the English to shuffle their jewelry.

When Lord Cornwallis returned to England, he found that neither the king nor his peers blamed him for losing the war. Instead, they were eager for

Queen Victoria never visited the jewel in her crown, and while she was in England being crowned Empress of India, this parallel ceremony was held in Delhi. If you contrast the crabbed and decaying London of "Gin Lane" on page 4 with this portrait of English rule in India 120 years later, you can see how empire gave England a sense of power and authority.

(KNEBWORTH ESTATES, WWW.KNEBWORTHHOUSE.COM)

him to take control of another trouble spot. Despite the government's reforms, the old abuses of East India Company control seemed to be going on as ever before. It was time to put the English territories in India in the hands of a single, strong, upright, moral leader who would be both governor and head of the army. The obvious choice was Lord Cornwallis. In 1786 the man whose defeat gave America its independence sailed off to ensure that India would come more firmly under English rule.

India was like the second daughter whose older sister had turned wild and fled from home. Her parents were determined not to let that happen again. While many company men came to India to make their fortunes and return home, others chose to remain. They might wear Indian clothing, which was much better suited to the heat than English dress. They might investigate and come to appreciate Hinduism, or even convert to Islam. Most of all, they might have Indian wives or mistresses. The children of these alliances were the beginning of something new—a mixed race of Anglo-Indians. Cornwallis was sent to India to bring order. The one thing he did not want was for India to become another America, where colonists began to sense their separation, their distance, from the homeland. Starting the year he arrived, one law after another banned the children of mixed marriages from working for the East India Company. India was to be a place that England ruled, not a new land in which the English were themselves transformed. Year by year through the first half of the nineteenth century, as more and more of India came under the sway of the company and the government, the character of English rule tightened.

Even as Cornwallis departed to govern India, a very different group of people in England were working to alter the entire foundation of the English Empire. George Whitefield, whose revivalist trips through America had played a part in bringing black and white worshipers together, was opposed to slavery. Hearing him speak in 1755, a man named John Newton, who had been the captain of a slave ship, decided that he had to change his life, and now he dedicated himself to preaching and to writing a book on the horrors of slavery. Nine years later a boy named William Wilberforce heard Newton speak—and found his life mission. Like Tom Paine, most Quakers were opposed to slavery, and they too joined the cause. But it was not until 1787, when an Anglican named Thomas Clarkson wrote a prize essay on slavery, that the movement to end the English slave trade really gathered force.

Dr. William Fullerton learned a number of Indian languages and had Indian mistresses. Here he is seen smoking an Indian pipe and seeming very relaxed. He was an Englishman becoming ever more Indian, which is the kind of behavior Cornwallis was determined to stop.

(IM. 33-1912, V&A IMAGES / VICTORIA AND ALBERT MUSEUM)

Early supporters of the cause included Thomas Babington and his brother-in-law Zachary Macaulay, whose son Thomas Babington Macaulay would later write the essay on Clive that was read by so many English and Americans.

Using all the methods of molding opinion through the press that Sam Adams and Laurence Sulivan had developed, and new ones more characteristic of modern public relations, the English abolitionists gathered thousands, then tens of thousands, of signatures on petitions to Parliament. They pressured businesses whose products were the products of slave labor with boycotts and protests, and honored those who could prove that they paid wages to their workers. They sent images of the holds of slave ships to newspaper editors, and confronted reporters with the instruments of torture used on board. By 1807 they had succeeded in banning the English slave trade, and on August 1, 1833, the enslaved peoples in the British Empire were freed. This date became a cherished anniversary of freedom for enslaved people in North America still awaiting their emancipation.

Ironically, while the American colonists fought a war against England to assert their independence, it was the English who first recognized that this need was universal and freed their slaves. Slavery was as old as human civilization, but forbidding it was completely new, and the English deserve the honor for being the first to recognize that it was also completely right to do so. Grenville had hoped to protect the Indians in America with his Proclamation Line. That failed in part because it never mattered enough to his fellow Englishmen. But in the emancipation movement the English showed that they could make the moral issue of the rights of oppressed people so important that it galvanized the nation—and changed history. They did this while also revising their election laws to allow Catholics to vote and to make Parliament more, but not very much more, representative.

If the challenge for Americans is to explain how they could build a nation on commitments to both democracy and slavery, for the English it is to understand how they could be the first to ban slavery while continuing to resist real democracy. The emancipation movement left England's economists with a great problem. How would the sugar, rice, and cotton crops of the English lands of the West Indies be harvested without slave labor? India provided the English with an answer. In an exact reverse of the pattern in colonial Virginia, indentured Asian Indians took the place of freed slaves in the fields of the great plantations.

One reason the English were able to find people willing to leave their homeland and venture across the "black water," the ocean, was that there had been a great convulsion in India. In 1857 the loyal Hindu and Muslim soldiers, who had done so much to win India for England, rebelled. Though the English were finally able to suppress the uprising, this marked the end of any flexibility in their rule. The East India Company lost its last measure of influence on India, and the government took over. It was this new phase of absolute English dominance that Queen Victoria celebrated twenty years later.

Indian soldiers who had lost in battle had an option—to leave the country for the Caribbean and work on the plantations. Being part of a world-spanning empire, though, also offered other opportunities for Indians: They could build railroads in Africa, they could open shops in Fiji, some could even study law in England.

In 1893 one young lawyer who had studied in England left India to serve the Indian community in South Africa. Mohandas K. Gandhi had been born in 1869, just as England's rule of India became absolute. Gandhi, though, was determined that his country should become independent. He admired the Americans for having gotten away, having made their escape. When he returned to India in 1915 and came to lead the movement to get the English to leave, he used the same techniques of nonimportation and encouraging people to weave their own cloth that had worked in the American colonies' struggle for independence.

Gandhi was a pacifist. Unlike Washington, he would never fight a war, even to lead his people to freedom. Instead, his campaign relied on moral force: the more violent, brutal, or irrational the British were in responding to his protests, the more support he garnered both in India and in the rest of the world. Then, in a twist that would seem unbelievable in a novel, history repeated itself.

In 1943 famine broke out in Bengal. In this case it was not because of lack of rain. Instead, it was an unintended but catastrophic consequence of wartime economic conditions. The British, who were buying rice for the soldiers fighting in World War II, and Bengalis, who had good incomes from working on wartime projects, drove the price of the grain so high that common laborers and farmers could no longer afford it. Since winning the war mattered more to the English than feeding the people, they did nothing to correct this. Weakened by hunger, between 1.5 and 3 million Bengalis fell victim to disease and starvation. In 1770, when the East India Company had taken over Bengal, millions died, and it soon had to concede some authority to the British government. And now, again, even as the people of India demanded their independence from that same government, a similar disaster was unfolding. The contrast between the callous British rule and Gandhi's sterling morality could not have been clearer. On August 15, 1947, India attained the freedom her American sister had won in 1783.

The long years of English dominance, though, had taught India, and especially Gandhi, something. The only way to fight a power such as England, which had vast superiority of weapons and control of the government, was through nonviolence. Like the English abolitionists, he used public opinion to force England to do what was morally right, no matter how otherwise unappealing. The power of well-organized nonviolence to undermine even the most cruel and violent rule was the message that India, the sister who was forced to submit, had to offer America, the sister who had broken free.

It took nearly a century, and a civil war, for Americans to cut through the knot that bound slavery with freedom. But the effects of slavery lingered long after. The racial attitudes that granted whites a sense of superiority were not changed by the Emancipation Proclamation. Instead, in many parts of the country they were enforced with the violence of Klans, lynch mobs, or segregated police departments. Any individuals who tried to challenge segregation in these areas faced the kind of organized, often deadly, fury that had brought English troops to Boston. But for almost another century no American president was willing to use federal troops to defend black rights. Though Americans fought heroically against Hitler in defense of democracy in World War II, there seemed no way to extend real rights to all Americans.

When he was a doctoral student at Boston University in the 1950s, the Reverend Martin Luther King Jr. learned of Gandhi and the great success of his nonviolent campaign. By

WIN PEACE & FREEDOM THRU NONVIOLENT ACTION

Martin Luther King
1929-1968

The virtues of mercy, nonviolence
love and truth in any man can
be truly tested only when they
are pitted against ruthlessness,
violence, hatred and untruth...
Mohandas K. Gandhi

WIN Magazine • 503 Atlantic Ave. • Brooklyn, NY 11217

In this 1968 poster Dr. King speaks just above a quotation from Gandhi.

(LIBRARY OF CONGRESS)

studying Gandhi, Dr. King found the tool that he could use in the violent South. Similarly, in the 1960s, when Cesar Chavez led the often abused Hispanic migrant workers of central California to fight for their rights, he found his inspiration in Gandhi's words and deeds. The moral power that forced England to give up India could work just as well to make America live up to its own principles. Paine had been more right than he knew. America's example did shine forth to the world. But America also needed to learn how to live up to its own promise from the rest of the world. For the Revolution in the minds of the people to truly be effective, it had to reach around the planet.

To My Readers, Again

The United States of America was born out of the union of thirteen colonies in which people were no longer content to be part of an empire. Since the fall of Communism in 1989, America has become the world's only superpower. This is the last and strangest sense in which our heritage from the colonial era is still playing out today. We have become the even more potent successor of the empire we overthrew. That is both our danger and our challenge. Can we learn from our own past, or are we going to inspire other nations to revolt, in one way or another, against us? In large part, that is up to readers of books like this.

No one is perfect, and it would be silly to expect America to handle its turn at global leadership flawlessly. For that matter, other nations and peoples will surely sometimes let their envy cloud their judgment of us. But I hope that looking at our past can at least sensitize you, future leaders, to the particular challenge of being American. Whether it was Sir Walter Ralegh lusting for the virgin lands that he also yearned to protect, John Winthrop hopelessly insisting that New Englanders *must* love one another, or the Founding Fathers roiling in their conflicts over slavery, the limitless horizons America presents have forced leaders to also face their limitations.

America is the canvas of human possibility, which also means of human weakness.

The danger of empire is arrogance, the assumption that a nation is better because it is stronger. It was that outlook that cost England first America, then India, then all its colonies. George Johnstone was removed from his job in West Florida in part because he was too proud to accept anyone else's authority. His first cousin James Murray lost his post as Royal Governor of Canada at just about the same time, and for similar reasons—he would not listen to anyone else. Johnstone was also one of the commissioners sent across the Atlantic in 1777 to see if the crown and the former colonies could negotiate a settlement. His arrogance and hot temper played an important part in ruining that last faint hope. Playing on the in-group networks of empire, the Johnstone clan ensconced itself in power, only to lose a good part of what it had won. In the end, the Johnstones inadvertently undermined the empire itself. John Wilkes, as it turned out, was exactly what his enemies had always claimed—a demagogue who would whip up popular feeling about issues, even though he had no principles of his own. After Parliament finally seated him in 1774, he abandoned his supporters in England and America and argued against the American Revolution.

Whether America's turn at global leadership will be filled with its own Johnstones, abusing power, its own Wilkeses, using popular protests for their own ends, or its own Wilberforces, establishing new possibilities for human freedom, is up to you. You have only the traces they left behind to guide you. I have drawn a map based on their explorations, but you will have to travel on it by yourselves.

ENDNOTES

To My Readers

p. xv   There is an excellent book for young readers that traces how views of American history have changed over time—Steven H. Jaffe's *Who Were the Founding Fathers?* (Complete bibliographical information on all works cited here will be found in the Bibliography, which starts on page 215.)

As I neared the end of my research for this book, I saw a footnote (number 14, on page 493) in C. A. Bayly's *The Birth of the Modern World, 1780–1914*, a very recent book that treats the period from 1780–1914 in a global way, not concentrating on just one country or region. The note cited a paper on "the East India Company and the American Revolution" that had recently been given at a conference.

The paper was written by Professor Emma Rothschild, an expert on the late eighteenth century who runs the Centre for History and Economics at Cambridge University in England. She is married to Amartya Sen, a Nobel Prize–winning economist from Bengal, who did pathbreaking research on the relationship between how democratic a nation's political system is and how severely that country suffers when it is struck by famine. As readers will discover, that background is directly relevant to the story she is researching. I contacted Professor Rothschild and learned that she is writing a book on precisely the topic I had stumbled upon. It was both disappointing and intimidating to realize that I was not alone in my discoveries, and that such a well-qualified and prominent scholar was well into her own study of this material. But it was also reassuring: It showed me that I was asking the right questions, and I was on the right track.

Professor Rothschild was kind enough to send me two articles relating to her research, and they hint at the depth of what she has discovered. But until her book is published, readers of this book who find the information in it strange or novel will have to consult the often extremely obscure sources in these notes. But that also means that at least the first readers of this book will have the pleasure of reading history that is really fresh and new before most anyone else knows it.

p. xvi   John Adams's line is frequently cited—for example, on page 1 of Bernard Bailyn's *The Ideological Origins of the American Revolution* (hereafter IO). Bailyn is one of the great scholars of the Revolution, and his book transformed the way in which the struggle was understood. He showed that the antigovernment pamphlets that many colonists were getting from England put them into an almost paranoid mindset that colored how they saw every action and statement from the English government. I give a very brief outline of his argument in Chapter 6. The book is part of the basic required reading for any serious college student, and it is aimed at that level. But as it was first published in 1967, its key insights have since been made available in many textbooks and other more popular books that are less academic in tone. When I was in graduate school, a group of Bailyn critics was on the rise, faulting him for paying too much attention to elite reading and not enough to the experiences of less literate and articulate members of American society. But then as now, I found his research compelling and his case convincing.

A slightly different version of the same quotation appears in the first part title, page 16, of David McCullough's Pulitzer Prize–winning biography, *John Adams* (hereafter JA). The book is written for adults, but it is a marvel of engaging writing. McCullough has mastered the art of using research, and only research, to make history vivid and immediate. Few young readers will read it all, but I highly recommend reading individual chapters for both the information and the writing. The one caution I have is that in order to get us to see Adams in a new light, McCullough takes every opportunity to contrast him with Thomas Jefferson. McCullough knew that readers would begin his book thinking much more highly of Jefferson, and he misses no chance to try to reverse our opinions. As a historian, I found some of the examples forced—more of an argument, a lawyer's case, than a fair account. I urge young readers to keep the author's point of view in mind, and to consult other sources on Adams before assuming that McCullough is always right, or Jefferson quite so wrong.

Three Soldiers:
Robert Clive, George Washington, and James Wolfe

Chapter 1: *First Soldier: From Despair to Conquest*

p. 3   Clive's childhood and background are discussed in every one of his biographies. But American readers are somewhat at a disadvantage in reading about him. English authors writing for an English audience assume that their readers already know at least his most famous battles, and that they have an opinion of him. Generations of English people from the mid-nineteenth century through at least the end of World War II were reared on the image of Clive as a great hero. One of the books that were most influential in creating that view was Thomas Babington Macaulay's *Essay on Lord Clive* (hereafter LC), which I discuss later in this chapter. It is one of those eminently readable and persuasive histories that the English wrote in the nineteenth century. The writing is still compelling—it reads like Rudyard Kipling or, if you prefer, the plot of a big-budget action movie—but the assumptions in it are very dated. G. A. Henty, whose books entertained generations of English and American schoolboys, translated Macaulay's Clive into a character in his 1884 novel *With Clive in India,* which made Clive popular not only as a person but as a heroic type that is still found in movies. As late as World War I, Macaulay was standard fare in both America and England. The edition I read, for example, was created in 1910 for American high school students. On the one hand the many explanatory notes it contains show that students no longer shared the same worldview as Macaulay, but the fact that the book was published indicates that schools still thought it was important for them to know his work.

More recently, though, both Macaulay and Clive have gone out of favor, as has the British Empire itself. So much so that there have been only a few recent biographies of Clive, and even those seemed to be fighting the old battles to raise or sink his place in history.

As an American coming to books about Clive without knowing much about him, and without a strong point of view about the British Empire, I often felt that the books were filled with assumptions I did not share, and that they were intended for other readers. Nonetheless, I did find books that were informed and well written, and included the kind of surrounding information that put his life into its context.

The first full biography of Clive I read was Percival Spear's *Master of Bengal* (hereafter MB), and that was fortunate. Spear was a scholar of British India, and so he was very skilled at surrounding Clive's life story with insights into society and culture. His book has a great many well-chosen black-and-white illustrations. His writing, though, is dry in places, and goes into more detail than any young reader will need. I was grateful to be directed to Mark Bence-Jones's *Clive of India* (hereafter CI) by a graduate student named Spencer Leonard, whose interesting research on the East India Company I found on the Internet. Vivid, colorful writing and a sober skepticism about many stories others have accepted make this the best biography of Clive that I found, though the illustrations in MB are far better. (Bence-Jones uses a turn of phrase on page 240 that is likely to offend many American readers but was considered acceptable by his English readership when he wrote the book.)

For Clive's youth and background and the England of his day, see MB, pages 11–22; for just Clive, see CI, pages 1–7.

p. 5   Casanova's remark appears on page 9 of Sheila O'Connell's catalog *London 1753*. Written to accompany an exhibition of the same name, it is a typically informative museum catalog, and I was fortunate to be in London for the show. The catalog is a very good place to look to get a sense of the London of that period, or to find illustrations for a report, but it is a reference tool, not a narrative history. The term "a Casanova"—meaning a seducer of women, a playboy—is taken from the real man, Giovanni Jacopo Casanova de Seingalt, who was, among other things, a diplomat and a spy, but was most famous for his romantic affairs. He is said to have advised

Lorenzo Da Ponte, the man who wrote the words for Mozart's opera *Don Giovanni*, which is about a Don Juan, a man very much like Casanova, and being a good sport, Casanova attended its first performance.

p. 5   Two very different books served as my guide to the history of the East India Company. Philip Lawson's *The East India Company: A History* (hereafter EIC) is a historian's crisp but balanced sifting of all the evidence, and all the studies, on the company's history. A short book, it is a terrific resource for getting information, and also for learning the pros and cons of the various interpretations. But it is aimed at college-aged readers. High school readers can best use it if they have begun to learn about the company and want to see if there are other points of view they should know. Lawson is very attuned to the criticisms of the company, and he has read all the relevant scholarship from India as well as England. But if there is a slant to the book, it is in a slight tone of regret that the company was not able to resist government control. Antony Wild's *The East India Company: Trade and Conquest from 1600* is a lavish coffee table book, filled with color illustrations. The author is a director of the surviving version of the East India Company, but his book is not at all defensive about the company's failings. The headquarters at Leadenhall Street are described on page 71. This is an appealing book for any reader.

p. 7   The best book I know on the history of Moguls for younger readers is Ed Rothfarb's *In the Land of the Taj Mahal*. It is an excellent way to begin to get to know this fascinating dynasty. The author has gone on to pursue a doctorate in the art history of this period of Indian history.

p. 8   Graphs comparing the temperatures of London and Madras are available at www.free-weather.com. I found the quotation about the furnacelike heat of Madras on page 21 of Franklin and Mary Wickwire's *Cornwallis and the War of Independence*. Readers wondering what a book with this title has to do with India will find answers in Chapter 14 of this book. I found the Wickwires' book while using Questia, an Internet library available by subscription. Questia is both a marvelous and a frustrating resource. It gives you online access to tens of thousands of books, including gems such as this quotation, which I would otherwise not have found. But the selection is erratic—for example, it sometimes has only one volume of a larger set. And many of the books are either quite dated or very recent and aimed at college-level readers. A younger reader is likely to have difficulty sorting through the books and figuring out which are best to use, and probably the best strategy is to ask a librarian or teacher for recommendations and then to cherry-pick through those available on Questia for interesting details and sidelights.

Ed Rothfarb told me about the ice in the New England ships, and I later found the story confirmed in other research. I am grateful to him for passing on that nice detail.

p. 10   All of Clive's writings about India, starting with his letters home from Madras, are remarkably silent about the sights and sounds of the world around him. There is something revealing in that—he saw power and opportunity, not peoples and cultures. He shows neither prejudice against India nor infatuation with it. He simply never chose to write about the temples, clothing, religions, or ideas he encountered. Biographers have pieced together his probable first impressions of Madras from general knowledge of the place and of his temperament. Spear's version, including the absence of women on the streets, can be found on pages 23 and 37–40 of MB. Like Spear, Bence-Jones lived in India, and his description of Clive's Madras reads like the best travel writing; see pages 9–10 and 16–17 of CI.

Clive's often quoted letter to his cousin appears in CI on page 11. Readers interested in Cromwell's alternations between melancholy and indefatigable determination can find my discussion of it on pages 99–101 of *John Winthrop, Oliver Cromwell, and the Land of Promise* (hereafter JW). Like most biographers of Clive, Spear tells the story of the two games of Russian roulette and Clive's subsequent sense of destiny; it appears on page 39 of MB. He says that Clive was "reported" to have done this, but he does not linger to question whether the story was true. Bence-Jones, on the other hand, thinks Clive was not as miserable in his early Madras days as other authors have claimed, and he explicitly does not believe the suicide story: see page 15 of CI. He points out in his footnote 42 on page 307 that it was first reported in a nineteenth-century biography as a well-known incident, with no further evidence. There is no doubt that Clive had bouts of depression and suicidal impulses. But the dramatic near misses followed by an intuition of his future destiny do sound so novelistic, they might well have been invented.

Spear lists some of Clive's reading, including Ralegh, on page 39; Bence-Jones also cites a number of the books available in the library Clive used, on page 17 of CI. I discuss the place of Ralegh's *History of the World* in Cromwell's life on page 101 of JW and the story of how that book was written on pages 177–79 of *Sir Walter Ralegh and the Quest for El Dorado* (hereafter SWR).

p. 11   The saga of the French in India is itself fascinating, and has many links with American and English history that I knew nothing about before I began this research. Readers who are curious can start with the truly unbelievable life story of a numbers whiz and farsighted economist named John Law, whose life took him from Scotland to a mysterious murder in London, to the gambling tables of Europe, to a role in completely transforming the French economic system, to a stock market frenzy called the South Sea Bubble that was actually based on the future value of Louisiana, to the founding of the French East India Company. He died in complete poverty, and the collapse of his policies is considered one of the long-range causes of the later French Revolution. A version of one of his ideas was also very important in American history, as trying to apply it to banking in Massachusetts got Sam Adams's father into financial and political difficulties that were crucial in shaping Sam's own devotion to the cause of independence. I researched Law on Questia, and through basic Internet searches.

Spear gives the background for Dupleix and Clive on pages 42–49 of MB, and Bence-Jones on pages 24–26 of CI. I assume there are many more books about Dupleix and the French East India Company in French, but in English an older work, Henry Dodwell's *Dupleix and Clive* is still used. I found it dishearteningly dusty and difficult to wade through.

p. 16   Macaulay's riveting account of the siege of Arcot runs from page 23 to 28 of LC; the storm is described on page 23. Both Spear and Bence-Jones assume their readers have grown up on Macaulay's version, and that they have to correct its romantic excesses before describing what actually took place. Spear's deflating account of a more confused battle that was significant mainly for Clive's impressive determination and sense of organization is on page 51 of MB; Bence-Jones's longer and more engaging version runs from page 39 to 49 of CI.

p. 19   Macaulay tells the story of the destruction of Dupleix's column on page 28 of LC. Bence-Jones in a thoughtful note shows that there is some doubt about whether the column had been fully set up when Clive arrived—see note 33 on page 314 of CI.

p. 20   I found a conversion table that gives the 2002 dollar equivalent for English pounds at various moments in the eighteenth century in Walter Isaacson's *Benjamin Franklin* (hereafter WIBF) on page 507. In 1750 one pound purchased about as much as 160 dollars in 2002. To make my conversions in this book, I have simply multiplied by 160. Including such a helpful resource is typical of the thoughtful presentation in this extremely well researched and user-friendly book. This is one biography any young reader should be able to use almost as an encyclopedia to look up reliable information about Franklin and his world. That said, I found Isaacson's interpretation of Franklin, and especially his argument that America was split between fierce Puritans such as Jonathan Edwards and pragmatists such as Franklin, simplistic to the point of being misleading. Any reader who has read JW will know that I believe Puritanism and pragmatism were intertwined in American history and were not complete opposites. I hope this does not sound like sour grapes, as his book was a mammoth bestseller, but he is much stronger on details than on a general sense of Franklin's time.

p. 21   This background material on representative government in Europe comes from Joseph Bergin's collection *The Seventeenth Century,* which is part of the Short Oxford History of Europe series. For the statistics on the percentage of people working the land, and the enforcement of serfdom in eastern Europe, see pages 18–19. This is a useful survey text that teachers or high-level advanced placement students can use as a resource.

Readers can find the sobering fact about the population in 1787 in Adam Hochschild's article "Against All Odds" (also on the web). This fascinating article on the English emancipation movement is being expanded into a book. I refer to it again in Chapter 14. I urge everyone to read the original, or the book when it comes out.

p. 22   For the telling description of Old Sarum go to http://www.historylearningsite.co.uk/first_past_the_post.htm, an educational site that explains the English voting system; see also http://dspace.dial.pipex.com/town/terrace/adw03/ c-eight/constitu/parlrep.htm for a more detailed discussion of how the English Parliament was elected in this period.

p. 23   The reason for hedging the description of the Earl of Sandwich's sexual activities is that he was said to be a member of something called the Hell-Fire Club, which I describe in more detail in Chapter 4. It is much easier to find rumors about this group than to know exactly what went on in its "meetings." It has been described as everything from a pagan cult to a relatively innocent club, which of course has encouraged sensational and fictional accounts. But in this period it was not unusual for someone like the Earl of Sandwich to be involved with prostitutes, and so even without knowing exactly what went on at the club, there is no reason to doubt that his reputation was deserved.

CHAPTER 2: *Second Soldier: Into the Forest*

p. 26   I know less about George Washington than I should, and therefore relied on one of the most established, reliable sources: James Thomas Flexner's *George Washington* (hereafter FGW), an extremely painstaking yet surprisingly readable book; Fred Anderson's *Crucible of War* (hereafter CW); and Edmund S. Morgan's short, insightful book *The Genius of George Washington*. Flexner is a traditional historian, clear and solid. Anderson gives fresh insight to every moment and represents the latest thinking on the crucial period he discusses. Morgan's book is a study, not a biography, but filled with interesting perceptions. All of these books would make good reference resources for motivated readers. My interpretation of Washington in this period is based on Anderson's.

p. 28   Flexner provides these examples of the *Rules* on page 22 of FGW. I am grateful to Professor Bender for stressing the irony of the difference between Washington's own character and that of the nation he did so much to establish.

p. 32   Go to http://www.users.mis.net/~chesnut/pages/gistjournal.pdf for

Christopher Gist's journal. I first learned of Gist in CW and simply used a search engine to learn more about him, which led to this fascinating document.

p. 32   My interpretation of Tanaghrisson's motives and actions follows from CW. Anderson has made more efforts than previous scholars to understand the Indians' points of view. For his account of the events in this chapter, see pages 5–65.

p. 35   CW quotes John Show's eyewitness account of this gruesome act on page 55. Gist quotes the New England woman in his journal, at the same site listed above.

p. 38   For information on Daniel Boone, including the quoted line in the subheading, I have relied on John Mack Faragher, *Daniel Boone* (hereafter DB); see page 38. I have retained the spelling "Britton" used in the book. Though written by a scholar for an adult audience, this is an engaging and readable modern account. Anyone who shares my fascination with Boone will enjoy this book, though the author does not hesitate to criticize Boone where appropriate.

CHAPTER 3: *The Heroes*

p. 41   The Dutch merchant is quoted in Nitish Sengupta, *History of the Bengali-Speaking People* (hereafter HBSP), on page 2. This book has the advantage of being published in India by a knowledgeable Bengali.

p. 42   For Macaulay's account of the Black Hole, see LC, page 41.

p. 42   I distinctly recall reading sensational accounts of the Black Hole as a child and did not know they had been challenged until I began working on this book. HBSP, page 142, describes the reasons for discounting Holwell's account and weighs the evidence for what actually took place. CI is similarly skeptical on page 91. The two books disagree in an interesting fashion on the character of Siraj. Relying on a French source who had no reason to make the nawab look bad, Sengupta argues that Siraj was responsible for exhibitions of cruelty such as having boatloads of people drowned in order to enjoy their agonies—see page 139. But CI argues that those reports were unlikely because they were not mentioned by Englishmen who had every reason to describe his worst traits—see page 89. So the Indian author, relying on an ally of Siraj's, describes him as cruel, while the Anglo-Irish author, relying on English sources, considers those reports implausible. All sources agree, however, that Siraj was a weak man facing a series of difficult choices.

p. 44   CI offers the name of the orchard and its translation. This description comes from an eyewitness account written by Clive's friend and ally Luke Scrafton, as quoted in Sir George Forrest's *The Life of Lord Clive*, volume one, on page 452. This hefty tome is, in modern terms, more a source book than a biography. It includes many long extracts from original documents but very little analysis. But it did give me access to primary sources, such as this one, that I could not have read in any other way.

p. 46   Clive's dealings with the merchant Omichand are a centerpiece of every biography. The fact that Clive had forged a signature and tricked Omichand were exposed in his time. Whether you view this as a grave failing, as Macaulay did (LC, pages 56–57), or as reasonable in view of the challenges of the time, as Bence-Jones does (CI, pages 128–30), will be a major element in how you evaluate him.

p. 48   Just as English authors writing about Clive assume readers know Macaulay's account, all historians of the conflict between the English and French in Canada write in the shadow of Francis Parkman. This nineteenth-century historian's account of the battle for Quebec is another classic of history, and was read by generations of American readers. I found Montcalm's confident line in a collection of Parkman's work, *Representative Selections*, edited by Wilbur L. Schramm (hereafter RS), page 468. This was a useful anthology that I found on Questia.

Anderson points out that Stobo himself is the only source for the story of his role in this battle but, in the end, thinks the account is believable; see CW, page 352. Not all scholars agree with Anderson about Stobo. For two highly readable books on the war that take a different view, see William Fowler, *Empires at War*, fn. 15, page 309, and Frank McLynn, *1759*, pages 295–97

p. 49   The interpretation of Wolfe as driven by his desire to die a heroic death is taken from Anderson—see CW, pages 353–59. For Parkman's quote, see RS, page 474. Anderson's comment on the same moment is that Wolfe's men "could hardly have relished the position into which their commander, ardent for any desperate glory," had thrust them. See CW, page 359. Historians such as Parkman and Macaulay believed moral character had a great deal to do with the outcome of historical events. Modern writers such as Anderson have less trust in these kinds of broad forces and pay more attention to each person's goals and motivations. Though I am not an expert on this period, I can imagine that some officers did find Wolfe's recital of Gray's "Elegy" inspiring, even if not terribly reassuring.

p. 51   On Clive's wealth, and the amount of the *jagir,* the annual payment, see CI, pages 188–89. For Amherst's views, see CW, pages 371–72.

Rights and Rules
Chapter 4: *Three Challenges*

p. 58   There are many books on the events in America in this period, and I relied on two as main sources. Robert Middlekauff is a highly respected historian of colonial America, and I recommend his *The Glorious Cause* (hereafter GC). John Ferling has also frequently written about the Founding Fathers, and I found useful details in his *A Leap in the Dark* (hereafter LD). Readers looking for a well-researched book aimed at a younger audience will find Albert Marrin's *The War for Independence* a good choice.

p. 59   Bernard Bailyn's *The Ordeal of Thomas Hutchinson* seeks to understand the outlook of the man whom people such as Sam Adams came to detest; for Bernard's background, see pages 45–46. It is another one of those standard college-level books that may be of interest to the advanced high school reader.

p. 60   Otis's ringing statement can be found in his 1764 *Rights of the British Colonies.* I read an excerpt in Samuel Eliot Morison, *Sources and Documents Illustrating the American Revolution, 1764–1788* (hereafter SAR), page 7. This is one of many such collections of original sources. Morison was immensely knowledgeable and was once considered a master of American history, but the point of view expressed in his notes in this book is quite dated—he identifies entirely with white Americans and has no interest in the Indians' point of view or experiences.

p. 62   For Adams's vivid description, see JA, page 62.

p. 63   Anderson's account of Neolin is on pages 536–38 of CW. I also used William R. Nester's *"Haughty Conquerors,"* which I found on Questia. Neolin is quoted on page 1. Anderson's thoughtful discussion of the use of smallpox blankets appears on pages 542–43 of CW. I found more information at Internet sites, including http://www.history.org/Foundation/journal/Spring04/warfare.cfm, which is an especially good article posted on the site of Colonial Williamsburg. Readers can see other versions of this same point about savagery in American history in SWR on page 72, and the section on the Pequot War on pages 75–80 of JW. That is how these books work as a trilogy: an incident between one Irish soldier and an Indian in the sixteenth century has commonalities with a war fought in the seventeenth century, and campaigns of terror and extermination in the eighteenth century—as well as with the actual efforts to kill or separate out all the remaining Indians in the nineteenth century. I was influenced in my interpretation by Bernard Bailyn's short book *The Peopling of British North America*, pages 116–18. Written to accompany a much longer, more detailed study, this summarizes many of Bailyn's important ideas and conclusions.

p. 65   As indicated earlier in the note to page 23, there are more stories and rumors about the Hell-Fire Club than certain knowledge. There is no doubt that the group of self-proclaimed "monks" existed, but we do not know exactly what they did in their meetings. Wilkes's famous quip can be found at http://dspace.dial.pipex.com/town/terrace/adw03/c-eight/people/wilkes.htm. This is a useful site, though it assumes the Hell-Fire stories were true and is otherwise more detailed than many readers will require. For Wilkes I relied on George Rudé, *Wilkes and Liberty* (hereafter WL), a well-known adult study that is as much about the world of the people affected by Wilkes as it is about his colorful life.

p. 67   For the crowd's cheer, see WL, page 26. For the story of the Levellers, their proposals, and Cromwell's response, see JW, pages 137–50.

CHAPTER 5: *London Responds*

p. 68   For the debts Grenville faced, see GC, page 57. The same numbers, along with the ridiculously small amount of customs revenue, are spelled out in Edmund S. Morgan and Helen M. Morgan, *The Stamp Act Crisis* (hereafter SAC). This is an older book by a great colonial historian and his wife, still readable and informative and the best place to begin research on this important thread in the buildup to the Revolution; see pages 21–23. This account of the tax burden on people in England and in North America comes from R. R. Palmer, *The Age of the Democratic Revolution*, pages 154–57. This is a classic adult study, which I was pleased to find on Questia.

p. 72   There is no biography and only one scholarly article on Sulivan, and a motivated young reader looking for a college-level research paper to write has an open field to correct that glaring absence, though the research is likely to require travel to archives in England, Ireland, and India, with no guarantees that there is anything new left to be found. For some current and balanced views, see CI, pages 193–96; MB, pages 128–30; EIC, pages 94–96.

p. 73   There is only one book on any of the Johnstones, and it focuses on George: Robin F. A. Fabel's *Bombast and Broadsides* (hereafter BB). It is an academic book, but the author is aware of the wild life his subject led and includes many colorful details. For George Johnstone's bravery and the filmic battle scenes, see pages 2–6. John Johnstone has no defenders, though BB is the most detailed and sympathetic—see pages 18–20; MB, 137; Bence-Jones faults Clive for being vindictive in his treatment of Johnstone—see CI, 212–14. All these books rely on another highly detailed study, which, to my great surprise and pleasure, turned out to be a wonderful book. That is Lucy S. Sutherland, *The East India Company in Eighteenth-Century Politics*. The book is a nearly day-by-day account of the machinations in the company and in Parliament during this period; it is both meticulously researched and a pleasure to read.

p. 75   It was William Pitt who praised Clive's heavenly leadership—see MB, page 93; for Townshend's remark, see MB, page 61; for Henry's stirring words, see GC, page 79.

CHAPTER 6: *Slave or Free?*

p. 78   Otis is quoted on page 34 of SAC, and the Assembly on page 35.

p. 78   The paragraph about the writings of the English skeptics is an extreme summary of Bailyn's detailed argument in IO. Readers curious to get a sense of the excitement that theory generated when it first came out, and who would like a brief outline of how later historians have engaged with it, should read Pauline Maier's introduction to the Norton paperback edition of her *From Resistance to Revolution* (hereafter RR).

p. 78   For Otis on Manchester, see IO, page 169. The suspicions of the Puritan ancestors are discussed throughout JW, but in particular on pages 32–34.

p. 80   John Adams on the Great Migration can be found in IO, page 140. The sense of the end of time is a theme throughout JW.

p. 82   For Townshend's speech, see GC, page 74.

p. 82   For Barré's response, see GC, page 75. I have retained the spelling (such as "'em" for "them") of this version.

p. 84   For the version of the French traveler's account that includes both the hangings and Henry's words, see SAC, pages 94–95.

p. 84   For Thacher's deathbed remark, see SAC, page 104.

p. 84   The great book on the colonial origins of this crucial knot in American life is Edmund S. Morgan's *American Slavery, American Freedom*. Like IO, this is a central book in our contemporary view of colonial history and a necessary read for any serious student of American history, though, again like IO, it was first published decades ago and its main arguments have long been incorporated by other authors.

p. 88   For Washington's views, see Henry Wiencek, *An Imperfect God*, especially pages 352–56. Author Jim Murphy graciously lent me his copy of the book, and his careful markings are a testimony to his fine research and clear thinking.

p. 88   For Jefferson's views, see E. M. Halliday, *Understanding Thomas Jefferson*, pages 141–53. Halliday points out how the chopped-off phrase from Jefferson's *Autobiography* entirely shifts its meaning. Many websites also make this point, and treat it as some form of propagandistic betrayal. And yet I think there is something to be said for a person who can articulate great ideas, even if his own thoughts contradict them. Authors can speak for all of us, even when they themselves are conflicted.

p. 90   Readers familiar with SWR will recognize that this paradoxical bond of greed and idealism was present from the first European explorations on—see pages 141–42.

CHAPTER 7: *Networks*

p. 91   I found these details on transportation in Richard B. Morris, ed., *Encyclopedia of American History* (hereafter EAH), a useful look-it-up resource that I often lean on for facts and dates; see pages 588–89. Though, as Vicki Smith helped me to learn, the book was wrong in a detail about roads in Maine.

p. 93   The Maryland paper is quoted, in all capitals, in SAC, page 100. For the Stamp Act Congress, see Merrill Jensen, *The Founding of a Nation*, page 123. This is a comprehensive older book that modern historians still rely on for a detailed and reliable account of events.

p. 94   The "spirit of democracy" quotation can be found in SAC, on page 110.

p. 94   The resolution appears on page 111, and the Massachusetts version on 118, of SAC.

p. 95   The story of MacIntosh, the Loyal Nine, and their organized violence is now a standard part of the story of the road to the Revolution. I used CW, pages 664–70; RR, pages 69–70; SAC, pages 127–28. For some historians crowd actions are particularly important because they are a way that people who left little or no written records influenced events and expressed some mixture of feeling and judgment. Books that look at MacIntosh and these events from that point of view include RR; Gary B. Nash, *The Urban Crucible*, pages 184–89; and Edward Countryman, *The American Revolution*, pages 101–3. For myself, I am more interested in ideas and articulate leaders than in violence and destructive mobs, no matter how planned and calculated their acts. Mobs may be the voice of the silenced people, but that voice is all too often one of rage, prejudice, and intimidation.

p. 99   Mayhew is quoted in Bernard Bailyn, *Faces of Revolution* (hereafter FR), page 131. This is a collection of interesting short essays, and the one on Mayhew's sermon would be useful for a student interested in the minister. The crowd is quoted in GC, page 92.

p. 100   The instruction to select plainer dresses can be found in SAC on page 33.

p. 101   Grenville is quoted in CW on page 655. Note this phrase when it comes up again in a different context on page 180. Franklin's sayings are quoted and discussed in WIBF—see especially page 99. While not as easy to use as Isaacson's biography, I preferred Edmund S. Morgan's short *Benjamin Franklin*.

p. 103   Pitt was renowned for his speeches, and it is worth reading the long extract in CW on pages 700–701 to get a sense of his eloquence and power; the line quoted appears on 701. Mason's response is quoted in GC on page 138.

CHAPTER 8: *Edges of Empire*

p. 106   This history is recounted in DB on pages 77–81.

p. 107   Captain Will is quoted in DB on page 81.

p. 108   Franklin's response to the Paxton Boys is quoted in WIBF on page 211. The rising tide of settlers is cited in CW on page 731.

p. 109   Washington's letter to the surveyor William Crawford can be found in FGW on page 292. Boone's comments are quoted and discussed in DB on page 144.

p. 111   Clive's letter is extensively quoted in MB on pages 145–48.

CRISIS

CHAPTER 9: *Half Measures*

p. 119   The story of the boom in East India stock, and its place in the history of world markets and world economic crises, can be found in David Glasner, ed., *Business Cycles and Depressions*. The entry on the Crises of 1763 and 1772–73 can be found on pages 112–23.

p. 120   When I began my research, I had never heard of this stock boom, and then I was fascinated to discover how it connected to American history. The Virginia side of the story is traced in T. H. Breen, *Tobacco Culture* (hereafter TC), a fine book on how the experience of growing, harvesting, and selling tobacco shaped the lives of the Virginia planters. See chapter 4, "The Loss of Independence," pages 124–59.

Horace Walpole's characteristically eloquent and contemptuous remarks can be found in Edward Lascelles, *The Life of Charles James Fox,* page 27. Questia happens to have many books from England that cover the people and events of this period in detail, and I trawled through them looking for details such as this. I found Pitt's telling words the same way, through a Questia search. They appear in A. Mervyn Davies, *Strange Destiny* (hereafter SD), on page 49.

The close connections of India hands and Parliament are spelled out in H. V. Bowen, *Revenue & Reform* on pages 30–33. This is an academic book that expands from Sutherland's book to a broader look at the interaction of India, the East India Company, and English politics. It is one of the newer books that are mapping out in detail the links among England, India, and the American Revolution that I sketch out in this book. MB, pages 176–77, names some of the returning India hands who were in Parliament and their allegiances.

p. 123   Bence-Jones talks more about Margaret than other biographers and seems to be the only researcher who investigated her social world. For Margaret and the snubbing of the Clives, see CI, pages 77, 169, 190.

p. 124   I found this revealing story, with another link to the Johnstones, on Questia; it is recorded in Dr. Alexander Carlyle's *Autobiography* on pages 147–48. Amazingly enough, John Wilkes was yet another schoolmate of theirs.

There is only one book-length study of Charles Townshend. It is a collection of writings on him started by the great English historian Sir Lewis Namier and completed after his death. The book includes the lecture in which Namier defines Townshend's character, speculates on why he behaved as he did, and relates this to his disastrous American policies. See "Charles Townshend, His Character and Career." I found the lecture at http://home.worldonline.co.za/~townshend/charles_townshend_lecture.htm. It is well worth reading. All American history textbooks discuss the Townshend Acts, but few describe the man behind them, and English books assume readers already know about his brilliance and quirks. This lecture was the only one I found that gave me a sense of who he was. Townshend is another good subject for an intrepid college-bound history major.

p. 126   Dickinson's "letters" are quoted and discussed in GC on pages 155–56. For "hot, rash," see the excerpt in SAR, page 43.

p. 127   Samuel Adams is described in LD on pages 60–64, in GC on pages 158–60.

p. 128   Ferling quotes Jefferson on Adams in LD on page 63.

p. 129   Bailyn quotes Franklin on Hillsborough and describes his motivations in FR, pages 174–76.

p. 129   Lloyd's journey is described in GC on page 185. I found Dickinson's words on page 70.

CHAPTER 10: *Liberty*

p. 133   The Boston papers are quoted in LD, page 73. The link between Wilkes and the Americans is explored in RR, chapter 6, pages 161–83; the details about naming are on page 163.

p. 135   Wilkes on "sacred Rights" can be found in RR on page 176. The ringing phrase about Wilkes and America can be found in IO on page 112. For nonimportation, see GC, pages 184–85, and EAH, page 92.

p. 137   For the efforts to intimidate and the objections from the merchant, see GC, pages 202 and 201 respectively. My account of the Boston Massacre follows GC, pages 203–8, and the quote is from 205.

p. 138   John Adams is quoted in JA on page 68.

p. 140   The ever witty and insightful Horace Walpole is quoted on the problems in governing India from London in EIC on page 107.

p. 140   This devastating and riveting account can be found at http://etext. library.adelaide.edu.au/f/fiske/john/f54u/chapter9.html./ As I understand it, this history, by a nineteenth-century English official named W. W. Hunter, is the only one ever written about the famine, which leaves another research project for the motivated student.

p. 141   Walpole is quoted in SD on page 65.

p. 142   Teachers interested in investigating these takes on the meaning of "liberty" will find John Phillip Reid's academic study *The Concept of Liberty in the Age of the American Revolution* useful. The similarity of the issues involved with regulating the East India Company and the American colonists is mentioned on page 86.

CHAPTER 11: *Tea*

p. 143   The subhead (repeated on page 147) is a quotation from John Adams in IO, page 98, footnote 3.

p. 144   The Fordyce story is yet another that has hardly been investigated by historians. I found the most information on him in Sir John Clapham, *The Bank of England*, pages 245–49, and Charles Wilson, *Anglo-Dutch Commerce & Finance in the Eighteenth Century*, pages 170–71. I have a strong sense that there is more to be learned about this fascinating gambler and his world—and since he was the direct cause of the crisis leading to the Boston Tea Party and thus the Revolution, we owe it to ourselves to know more about him.

p. 144   The story of the connection between the financial crisis of 1772 and the Revolution has been researched and spelled out in Richard B. Sheridan, "The British Credit Crisis of 1772 and the American Colonies." As obscure as this 1960 article is, first published in the *Journal of Economic History*, it makes a crucial bridge between American history and world history that should be present in every history of the Revolution. In TC, Breen discusses the effect of the bankruptcies in chapter 5, pages 160–203.

p. 146   Ferling discusses Washington's letter in LD on pages 82–84; the quotation appears on page 84.

pp. 149–53 My account of Clive and Parliament follows CI, pages 279–87; Walpole is quoted on page 281, Clive's longer speech on 286, and the shorter on 287. On that page Bence-Jones also wonderfully evokes the moment when Clive heard the verdict. I have gratefully followed his scene setting. Admiral Saunders is quoted on page 288. Those interested in the Ralegh trial can find out more about it in chapter 14 of SWR, pages 161–75.

p. 153   Clive's sense of his treatment by Parliament can be found in CI on page 281.

p. 155   Clive's feelings about the Americans and the rumor about his possible role in fighting against them are discussed in CI on page 296.

p. 158   There is only one scholarly book on the Tea Party: Benjamin Woods Labaree, *The Boston Tea Party* (hereafter BTP); for the warning to North, see page 71. This is a readable and well-researched older book that a motivated high school student can use for writing reports, though he or she has to be willing to sift through a detailed narrative. The count of chests and pounds of tea can be found in BTP on page 77.

CHAPTER 12: *Intolerable*

p. 159   This account of the actual Tea Party also follows BTP, chapter 7, pages 126–45.

p. 160   The scene in the church can be found in BTP on page 141.

p. 163   This participant's account can be found in Alfred F. Young, *The Shoemaker and the Tea Party*, a book that is as much about memory, recollection, and how events change from personal experiences into historical moments as it is about the Tea Party. See page 44 for the extract; Adams is quoted in BTP on page 145.

p. 165   For Jefferson's and Washington's words, see IO, page 120; Allen is quoted on page 122.

p. 166   The resolution appears in GC on page 249.

CHAPTER 13: *Common Sense*

p. 167   I used two main sources to develop my thinking on Paine. One was the older but still standard book by Eric Foner, *Tom Paine and Revolutionary America* (hereafter TPRA); the other was Bailyn's essay on Paine in FR, chapter 4, pages 67–84. Anyone interested in Paine should read Foner's book, which aims to show the relationship between Paine and other radicals of his time, though I also think it is time for a fresh look at him. *Common Sense* is easily available on the Internet—for example, at http://www.constitution.org/civ/comsense.htm. The quotation used as the sub-head here is used the same way in the Bailyn essay, see page 67.

Paine's essay "African Slavery in America" includes the quoted line. It was written in 1774 and published in March of the following year. It is available at http://www.thomaspaine.org/Archives/afri.html, a site that has many of his other writings, including his essay on the death of Lord Clive and, again, *Common Sense*. (I have not supplied page numbers for the quotations from *Common Sense*, since you cannot search by page in these online formats but rather by scrolling down.)

p. 168   The link between the Levellers and the Quakers is covered in JW on pages 156–59. The paragraph about Paine and rage is based on Bailyn's argument—see especially pages 82–83.

p. 170   For the early report on America, see SWR, pages 61–63; see also pages 133–42 for the ways in which Ralegh himself wrote of, and thought of, the New World as untouched and perfect—as well as ripe for conquest. For Winthrop, see JW, pages 39–41.

p. 171   The sense in which the Middle Atlantic colonies, which are usually given a minor role in the story of the formation of America, were actually better predictors of the nation's future than either Virginia or New England was one of the lessons I learned in graduate school from Dr. Bender.

p. 172   The astonishing publishing history of *Common Sense* can be found in TPRA on page 79. Ferling mentions Washington's instructions in LD on page 151.

p. 176   Bailyn points out the importance of this growth in the American population in FR, pages 164–65.

p. 179   Readers who would like to see how the international approach I have taken in this book applies to the battles of the Revolution can turn to Brendan Morrissey, *The American Revolution*. I was pleased to find this book after I completed mine, and it provides the perfect extension of my view of history to the actual battles of the Revolutionary War.

CHAPTER 14: *Revolutions*

p. 180   This ceremony is described in Lawrence James, *Raj: The Making and Unmaking of British India,* on pages 316–17. This is a readable, confident one-volume history filled with engaging incidents and factual details that any young reader can use for reference, though the point of view is English and the student would be advised to look at books from India, or by historians, for other perspectives on the people and events the author discusses.

p. 182   The fascinating and tragic history of the phase in which the English and Indians intermarried, had children, and began to form a combined culture is described in lush detail and novelistic episodes in William Dalrymple, *White Mughals,* certainly written for adults but a real treasure full of unexpected stories and fresh insights for motivated readers.

p. 182   These details of the English antislavery campaign are taken from the article cited in the note to page 21.

p. 185   My wife, whose father came from Guyana, informed me about the term "black water."

TO MY READERS, AGAIN

p. 190   Anderson describes the colonial experiences of these two cousins on pages 730–31 of CW.

BIBLIOGRAPHY

Anderson, Fred. *Crucible of War: The Seven Years' War and the Fate of Empire in British North America, 1754–1766*. New York: Vintage, 2001; abbreviated in the notes as CW.

Aronson, Marc. *John Winthrop, Oliver Cromwell, and the Land of Promise*. New York: Clarion, 2004; abbreviated in the notes as JW.

———. *Sir Walter Ralegh and the Quest for El Dorado*. New York: Clarion, 2000; abbreviated in the notes as SWR.

Bailyn, Bernard. *Faces of Revolution: Personalities and Themes in the Struggle for American Independence*. New York: Vintage Books, 1992; abbreviated in the notes as FR.

———. *The Ideological Origins of the American Revolution*. Cambridge, Mass.: The Belknap Press of Harvard University Press, 1967; abbreviated in the notes as IO.

———. *The Ordeal of Thomas Hutchinson*. Cambridge, Mass.: The Belknap Press of Harvard University Press, 1974.

———. *The Peopling of British North America: An Introduction*. New York: Vintage Books, 1988.

Bayly, C. A. *The Birth of the Modern World, 1780–1914: Global Connections and Comparisons*. Oxford, England: Blackwell Publishing Ltd., 2004.

Bence-Jones, Mark. *Clive of India*. London: Constable and Company, 1974; abbreviated in the notes as CI.

Bergin, Joseph, ed. *The Seventeenth Century: Europe, 1598–1715*. Series The Short Oxford History of Europe. Oxford, England: Oxford University Press, 2001.

Bowen, H. V. *Revenue & Reform: The Indian Problem in British Politics 1757–1773*. Cambridge, England: Cambridge University Press, 1991; page citations are to the 2001 paperback edition.

Breen, T. H. *Tobacco Culture: The Mentality of the Great Tidewater Planters on the Eve of the Revolution*. Princeton, N.J.: Princeton University Press, 1985; 9th ed. with new preface, 2001; page citations are to the 2001 edition; abbreviated in the notes as TC.

————. *The Marketplace of Revolution: How Consumer Politics Shaped American Independence*. New York: Oxford University Press, 2004.

Carlyle, Alexander. *Autobiography of the Rev. Dr. Alexander Carlyle, Minister of Inveresk: Containing Memorials of the Men and Events of His Time*. Boston: Ticknor and Fields, 1861.

Clapham, Sir John. *The Bank of England: A History*. New York: Macmillan Company, 1945.

Countryman, Edward. *The American Revolution*. New York: Hill and Wang, 1985.

Dalrymple, William. *White Mughals: Love and Betrayal in Eighteenth-Century India*. New York: Viking Books, 2003.

Davies, A. Mervyn. *Strange Destiny: A Biography of Warren Hastings*. New York: G. P. Putnam's Sons, 1935; abbreviated in the notes as SD.

Dodwell, Henry. *Dupleix and Clive: The Beginning of Empire*. London: Methuen & Co. Ltd., 1920. I used a more recent reprint edition, New Delhi: Asian Educational Services, 1989.

Fabel, Robin F. A. *Bombast and Broadsides: The Lives of George Johnstone*. Tuscaloosa, Ala.: University of Alabama Press, 1987; abbreviated in the notes as BB.

Faragher, John Mack. *Daniel Boone: The Life and Legend of an American Pioneer*. New York: Henry Holt, 1992; abbreviated in the notes as DB.

Ferling, John E. *A Leap in the Dark: The Struggle to Create the American Republic*. New York: Oxford University Press, 2003; abbreviated in the notes as LD.

Flexner, James Thomas. *George Washington: The Forge of Experience (1732–1775)*. Boston: Little, Brown and Company, 1965; abbreviated in the notes as FGW.

Foner, Eric. *Tom Paine and Revolutionary America*. New York: Oxford University Press, 1976; abbreviated in the notes as TPRA.

Forrest, Sir George. *The Life of Lord Clive*. 2 vols. London: Cassell and Co., 1918.

Fowler, William. *Empires at War: The French and Indian War and the Struggle for North America, 1754–1763*. New York: Walker & Company, 2005.

Glasner, David, ed. *Business Cycles and Depressions: An Encyclopedia*. New York: Garland, 1997.

Halliday, E. M. *Understanding Thomas Jefferson*. New York: HarperCollins, 2001.

Henty, G. A. *With Clive in India*. New York: Scribner and Welford, 1887.

Hochschild, Adam. "Against All Odds," in *Mother Jones*, January/February 2004. http://www.findarticles.com/p/articles/mi_m1329/is_1_29/ai_112087893.

Isaacson, Walter. *Benjamin Franklin: An American Life*. New York: Simon & Schuster, 2003; abbreviated in the notes as WIBF.

Jaffe, Steven H. *Who Were the Founding Fathers?: Two Hundred Years of Reinventing American History*. New York: Henry Holt, 1996.

James, Lawrence. *Raj: The Making and Unmaking of British India*. New York: St. Martin's Press, 1998.

Jensen, Merrill. *The Founding of a Nation: A History of the American Revolution, 1763–1776*. New York: Oxford University Press, 1968.

Labaree, Benjamin Woods. *The Boston Tea Party*. Oxford, England: Oxford University Press, 1964; reprint Boston: Northeastern University Press, 1979; page citations are to the Northeastern reprint edition; abbreviated in the notes as BTP.

Lascelles, Edward. *The Life of Charles James Fox*. New York: Oxford University Press, 1936.

Lawson. Philip. *The East India Company: A History*. London: Addison Wesley Longman, 1987; page citations are to 1993 reprint edition; abbreviated in the notes as EIC.

Macaulay, Thomas Babington. *Macaulay's Essay on Lord Clive*. Edinburgh, Scotland: The Edinburgh Review, 1840; page citations are to a later edition designed for American high school readers, edited with notes and an introduction by the then head of the English department at New York's Erasmus Hall High School, Preston C. Farrar. New York: Longmans, Green and Co., 1910; abbreviated in the notes as LC.

McCullough, David. *John Adams*. New York: Simon & Schuster, a Touchstone Book, 2001; abbreviated in the notes as JA.

McLynn, Frank. 1759, *The Year Britain Became Master of the World*. New York: Atlantic Monthly Press, 2005.

Maier, Pauline. *From Resistance to Revolution: Colonial Radicals and the Development of American Opposition to Britain, 1765–1776*. New York: Alfred A. Knopf, 1972; Norton paperback, 1991; pages cited are to the Norton edition; abbreviated in the notes as RR.

Marrin, Albert. *The War for Independence: The Story of the American Revolution.* New York: Atheneum, 1988.

Middlekauff, Robert. *The Glorious Cause: The American Revolution, 1763–1789.* New York: Oxford University Press, 1982; abbreviated in the notes as GC.

Morgan, Edmund S. *American Slavery, American Freedom: The Ordeal of Colonial Virginia.* New York: W. W. Norton, 1975.

————. *Benjamin Franklin.* New Haven: Yale University Press, 2002.

————. *The Genius of George Washington.* New York: W. W. Norton, 1977.

————, and Helen M. Morgan. *The Stamp Act Crisis: Prologue to Revolution.* Chapel Hill, N.C.: University of North Carolina Press, 1953; rev. ed. with new preface, 1995; pages cited are to the later edition; abbreviated in the notes as SAC.

Morison, Samuel Eliot. *Sources and Documents Illustrating the American Revolution, 1764–1788.* New York: Oxford University Press, 1965, 2nd ed; abbreviated in the notes as SAR.

Morris, Richard Brandon, ed. *Encyclopedia of American History.* New York: Harper & Row, 1953; 6th ed., 1982; pages cited are to the 6th edition; abbreviated in the notes as EAH.

Morrissey, Brendan. *The American Revolution: The Global Struggle for National Independence.* London: Salamander Books, 2001.

Namier, Sir Lewis. *Charles Townshend.* New York: St. Martin's Press, 1964.

Nash, Gary B. *The Urban Crucible: The Northern Seaports and the Origins of the American Revolution.* Cambridge, Mass.: Harvard University Press, 1979.

Nester, William R. *"Haughty Conquerors": Amherst and the Great Indian Uprising of 1763.* Westport, Conn.: Praeger Publishers, 2000.

O'Connell, Sheila. *London 1753.* London: British Museum Press, 2003.

Palmer, R. R. *The Age of the Democratic Revolution: A Political History of Europe and America, 1760–1800.* Princeton, N.J.: Princeton University Press, 1959.

Parkman, Francis. *Representative Selections,* edited by Wilbur L. Schramm. New York: American Book Company, 1938; abbreviated in the notes as RS.

Reid, John Phillip. *The Concept of Liberty in the Age of the American Revolution.* Chicago: University of Chicago Press, 1988.

Rothfarb, Ed. *In the Land of the Taj Mahal: The World of the Fabulous Mughals.* New York: Henry Holt, 1998.

Rothschild, Emma. "Globalization and the Return of History," in *Foreign Policy,* Summer 1999, pages 106–16.

Rudé, George. *Wilkes and Liberty: A Social Study of 1763 to 1774.* Oxford, England: Clarendon Press, 1962; abbreviated in the notes as WL.

Sengupta, Nitish. *History of the Bengali-Speaking People.* New Delhi: UBS Publishers' Distributors, 2001; abbreviated in the notes as HBSP.

Sheridan, Richard B. "The British Credit Crisis of 1772 and the American Colonies," in *Journal of Economic History,* volume XX, June 1960, pages 161–86.

Spear, Percival. *Master of Bengal: Clive and His India.* London: Thames and Hudson, 1975; page citations are to the Purnell Book Services Book Club Edition, London, nd; abbreviated in the notes as MB.

Sutherland, Dame Lucy S. *The East India Company in Eighteenth-Century Politics.* Oxford, England: Oxford University Press, 1952.

Wickwire, Franklin and Mary. *Cornwallis and the War of Independence.* Chapel Hill, N.C.: University of North Carolina Press, 1980.

Wiencek, Henry. *An Imperfect God: George Washington, His Slaves, and the Creation of America.* New York: Farrar, Straus, and Giroux, 2003.

Wild, Antony. *The East India Company: Trade and Conquest from 1600.* New York: The Lyons Press, 2000.

Wilson, Charles. *Anglo-Dutch Commerce & Finance in the Eighteenth Century.* Cambridge, England: Cambridge University Press, 1941; reprinted New York: Arno Press, 1977; page citations are to Arno reprint edition.

Young, Alfred F. *The Shoemaker and the Tea Party: Memory and the American Revolution.* Boston, Mass.: Beacon Press, 1999.

WEB SITES

(caption, page 181) http://www.knebworthhouse.com.
   Knebworth House has a site devoted to the castle and its collections, as well as the rock concerts that are held there. A fun site that is worth exploring.
http://www.free-weather.com.
   Free-Weather.coms's useful site offers graphs tracing the weather in locations throughout the world, making it very easy to compare climates.
http://articles.findarticles.com/p/articles/mi_m1329/is_1_29/ai_112087893.
   Findarticles.com makes available many magazine articles that would be difficult to locate outside of a well-stocked library. This url will lead you to Adam Hochschild's excellent article on the anti-slavery moment in England.
http://www.historylearningsite.co.uk/first_past_the_post.htm.
   Historylearningsite.co.uk is a good resource for information on the British political system and its history. You can click on many terms to learn more about them.
http://dspace.dial.pipex.com/town/terrace/adw03/c-eight/constitu/parlrep.htm.
   This url redirects the viewer to historyhome.com, a web outline of British history, with links to other useful sites.
http://www.users.mis.net/~chesnut/pages/gistjournal.pdf.
   If you have trouble reaching the URL listed here, type "Christopher Gist Journal" into any good search engine and it will take you to this PDF file.
http://www.history.org/Foundation/journal/Spring04/warfare.cfm.
   History.org, the Colonial Williamsburg site, contains a great deal of useful information on this period for all ages, including this thoughtful article on germ warfare.
http://dspace.dial.pipex.com/town/terrace/adw03/c-eight/people/wilkes.htm.
   This entry on Wilkes is a page within the Historyhome site listed above.
http://home.worldonline.co.za/~townshend/charles_townshend_lecture.htm.
   Home.worldonline.co.za is a site devoted to the history of the Townshend family. The complete text of Namier's lecture and essay on Townshend is a page within the site.

http://etext.library.adelaide.edu.au/f/fiske/john/f54u/chapter9.html./

I found the only history of the famine by using Google, which led me to this page. This site is not otherwise devoted to India or the history of this period.

http://constitution.org/civ/comsense.htm.

Constitution.org is one of many sites that offers the complete text of Common Sense.

http://www.thomaspaine.org/Archives/afri.html.

I found my way to Paine's early essay on abolition by going to Thomaspaine.org, then looking through his writings for his essays. This is a good site to make use of if you would like to read more of his work.

YEAR	ENGLAND/EUROPE
1741	
1743	
1744	
1746	
1748	Treaty of Aix-la-Chapelle—England and France at peace
1751	
1753	
1754	Clive gains seat in Parliament, election result overturned
1755	
1756	Seven Years' War officially begins
1757	
1758	
1759	
1760	George II dies, George III new king
1761	Clive elected to Parliament, Lord Bute made minister
1762	
1763	Peace of Paris ends Seven Years' War Clive and Sulivan begin battle for control of East India Company John Wilkes publishes *North Briton* #45, criticizing Lord Bute and the king; is arrested, released Lord Bute resigns, George Grenville leads government; new proposals for America include Proclamation Line and better customs inspection
1764	Wilkes is removed from Parliament; large protests; he flees to France
1765	Parliament passes Stamp Act Grenville resigns, replaced with Lord Rockingham Boom in East India Company stock

	NORTH AMERICA	INDIA
		J. F. Dupleix becomes governor of French-controlled town of Pondicherry, near Madras
	Thomas Jefferson born	
		Clive lands in Madras, possibly suicidal
		Madras captured by French
		Clive appointed quartermaster
		Clive triumphs in siege of Arcot
	Washington on mission to find French commandant	Clive marries, leaves for England
	Governor Dinwiddie orders fort built near modern Pittsburgh	
	French capture site and build own Fort Duquesne	
	Tanaghrisson, with Washington, kills French commander	
	Washington trapped, surrenders on July 4	
	Albany Plan, proposed union of colonies, rejected	
	General Braddock defeated, killed; Washington, Boone escape	Clive returns to India
		Siraj Ud-Daula drives English out of Calcutta; "BlackHole"
		Clive retakes Calcutta, wins at Plassey; Mir Jafar, new nawab, grants Clive annual payment
	Brigadier General John Forbes takes back Fort Duquesne	Clive appointed governor of Bengal
	Brigadier General James Wolfe takes Quebec, killed in battle; Major Isaac Barré injured on Plains of Abraham	
	French surrender Canada to English	Clive returns to England, named Baron Clive of Plassey
	Francis Bernard appointed governor of Massachusetts	
	James Otis argues against writs of assistance, "child Independence born"	
	Neolin begins telling of his journey to the land of spirits	
	Pontiac's Rebellion	
	George Johnstone appointed governor of West Florida	
	James Murray appointed governor of Canada	
	Patrick Henry argues that king cannot act illegally	
	Paxton Boys murder, riot	
		Clive appointed governor and commander in chief in Bengal
	Virginia House of Burgesses adopts Patrick Henry's resolutions against Stamp Act	Clive accepts grant of control of Bengal, Bihar, and Orissa from Shah Alam II
	Organized riots in Boston against Stamp Act	Clive clashes with John Johnstone
	Stamp Act Congress meets	
	Nonimportation movement in colonies	

YEAR	ENGLAND/EUROPE
1766	Stamp act rescinded, but Declaratory Act passed
	Lord Rockingham resigns, William Pitt holds power but is ill
1767	Charles Townshend proposes payment from East India Company and new taxes on Americans, Parliament approves; Townshend dies, Lord North replaces him
1768	Wilkes returns, is elected to Parliament, arrested
1769	Wilkes reelected, Parliament bars him; he is reelected again, election voided; he defeats Colonel Luttrell for seat in Parliament by large majority
	Fall in East India Company stock
1770	Colonel Luttrell seated in Parliament
	Lord North named Prime Minister
	All Townshend duties removed except tax on tea
1772	Alexander Fordyce flees to Europe, Ayr Bank collapses
	European credit crisis
	East India Company unable to pay its bills
	Parliament begins investigation of East India Company
1773	Colonel John Burgoyne's secret committee investigates Clive, but Parliament commends him
	Regulating Act offering East India Company loan and taking control of its territories in India passes
	East India Company given right to export tea to America without paying tax in order to repay government loan
1774	Intolerable Acts passed
	Clive commits suicide
	Wilkes elected again, allowed to take his seat in Parliament
1775	
1776	
1777	
1781	
1783	
1786	Sulivan dies
1787	Abolitionist movement gathers strength in England; George Johnstone dies
1790	
1797	Wilkes dies
1799	
1803	

NORTH AMERICA	INDIA
John Dickinson's "Farmer's Letters" published Nonimportation movement revived	Clive collapses, returns to England
At urging of Samuel Adams, Massachusetts legislature sends letter to other colonies protesting Townshend Acts *Liberty*, boat owned by John Hancock, seized English troops in Boston	
Daniel Boone crosses Cumberland Gap, hunts in rich lands, captured, warned, freed Nonimportation movement grows	Haidar Ali threatens Madras
Boston Massacre Nonimportation collapses	Famine in Bengal—millions die
Boston Tea Party	
Paine arrives in America First Continental Congress	
Battles of Lexington, Concord, and Bunker Hill Washington named leader of American army *Common Sense* published Declaration of Independence Burgoyne surrenders at Saratoga French recognize American independence Cornwallis surrenders to Washington England, France, and United States sign peace treaty	
	Cornwallis sent to govern English-controlled regions of India
Franklin dies	
Washington dies Samuel Adams dies	

YEAR	ENGLAND/EUROPE
1807	England bans slave trade
1820	
1826	
1832	England reforms rules for election to Parliament
1833	England bans slavery
1857	
1863	
1877	Queen Victoria named Empress of India
1943	
1947	
1955	

	NORTH AMERICA	INDIA
	Paine dies	
	Boone dies	
	John Adams and Jefferson die on July 4th, 50th anniversary of the Declaration they crafted (with Franklin)	
		Indian soldiers revolt, defeated by English; all East India Company authority in India ends
	Emancipation Proclamation in America	
		Famine in Bengal
		India achieves independence
	Dr. Martin Luther King Jr. leads boycott of segregated buses in Montgomery, Alabama	

INDEX

Note: Page numbers in *italic* type refer to illustrations.

England (*cont.*)
  kings of, 170–71
  Norman Conquest of, 21
  Parliament in, *see* Parliament
  at Quebec, 47–51
  slaves freed in, 182–85
  social conditions in, *4*, 5, *69*, 181
  taxes imposed by, 68–71, 77–78, 81–82,
    83–84, 93, *93*, 94–95, 100, 103,
    125–27, 133, 143, 158, 160

Fairfax, Thomas, 27
Findley, John, 106–7
Forbes, John, 47
Fordyce, Alexander, 144, *145*, 146
Fort Duquesne, Ohio, *34*
Fort St. George, Madras, 9, *14*, 20
France:
  and America, 31–32, *34*, 35, 47, 48–51,
    52, 53
  and American Indians, 32, 35–36, 38, 62
  and American Revolution, 177–78, *179*
  England vs., 33–36, *37*, 38, 39, 178, *179*
  and India, 11, 14, *14*, 15, 42
  at Quebec, 48–51
Franklin, Benjamin, 95, *102*
  and the economy, 77, 94, 143
  in England, 101, 129, 167
  and France, 177, *178*
  and independence, 165, 176, *177*

Franklin, Benjamin (*cont.*)
  and mob violence, 108
  Poor Richard's Almanac by, 101, 103
  and unity, 92
French East India Company, 14, 15
Fullerton, William, *183*

Gainsborough, Thomas, portrait by, *15*
Galloway, Joseph, 165, 166
Gandhi, Mohandas K. (Mahatma),
    185–86, 187–88
George III, king of England, 32, 60, 65, 101
"Gin Lane" (Hogarth), *4*
Glorious Revolution, 21
Gray, Thomas, 49
Grenville, George, 68–71, 77–83, 88
  loss of power by, 101
  and Proclamation Line, 71, 108–9, 184
  and taxes, 71, 81, 83, 93, *93*, 94–95, 97,
    99, 100, 125, 127, 158
Guy Fawkes Day, 95

Haidar Ali, 140
Hancock, John, 131
Hell-Fire Club, 65
Hemings, Sally, 89
Henry, Patrick, 76, 84, *85*, 128, 165
Hillsborough, Wills Hill, Lord, 129–30
Hogarth, William, 54, 96
  engravings by, *4, 23, 66, 69*